Unexpected Journey:

Fire and Gold

By

Dedrick L. Moone

and

Haelee P. Moone

The Rules of a Big Boss LLC
Knightdale, NC 27545

Dedication

I dedicate this memoir to my daughter, Haelee P. Moone. God gave me the gift of fatherhood, unconditional love, a roll dawg, and a best buddy on the day you were born. Your bravery in sharing your testimony in The Rules of a Big Boss: A book of self-love gave me the strength to share our story. You are my she-ro. I pray that the lessons that I have conveyed to you carry you forward in your journey. I pray that you see and receive this expression of love from me to you.

To you, yes, you. You have been through a lot, but you are still standing. I pray that this memoir, our memoir encourages and strengthens you to keep pushing. You CAN, and you WILL make it!

Table of Contents

Introduction

I have been through a litany of ups and downs. Some of those ups include unexpected promotions and bonuses. Some of those downs include employer retaliation and discrimination.

Those ups were my foundation. They birthed in me an even greater strength for the tough times that were ahead. In contrast, the downs served as a catalyst to strengthen me. I count it all joy because everything in life has a purpose. A semblance of that purpose is in my and Haelee's ability to share my and our experiences with readers, like yourself in this memoir. We write it to encourage you. Please know that tough times only make you stronger.

I hope that you are inspired having read this memoir. Thank you for your purchase and may it be a blessing to you.

CHAPTER 1: The Career Change

My major in Electronics Engineering and Information Technology in undergraduate school allowed me to start my career as an IT Specialist. The field required that I remain up to date on my technical knowledge, skills, and abilities. While I initially enjoyed it, I lost interest in late 2009. It no longer spoke to my heart and what was most important to me. Each day felt more like a burden than a pleasure until it was merely something that I was great at doing yet hated. I began to realize that I had chosen the wrong path for my career. Depression began to set in over time. Notwithstanding, I did what any wise person would do under those circumstances in that I started planning and praying for new beginnings.

My new beginning arrived in May 2010 and boy was I excited. I accepted a position as a Program Manager with a prestigious federal agency. Alas, the answer to my prayers. I finally had a job that was more strategic than it was technical, talk about flexibility. I could interact with people across various platforms and knowledge bases within and beyond that Agency. My new manager, Mr. McDonald, had an open mind, and he was huge on autonomy. He afforded me a great deal of creative ingenuity to get my work done. What's more, he would often say, "family first" because he was a family man. Mr. McDonald allowed my colleagues and myself to telework up to three days per week while encouraging community involvement through volunteering and mentoring within our local community.

The program office accomplished a great deal during that time. Some of those accomplishments have been key highlights within my career. At any rate, Mr. McDonald served as my first line supervisor until the summer of 2013. The program office was reassigned to the Chief of Staffs (CoS) Office during that time. It had previously operated under the Chief Information Officer (CIO). Mr. McDonald was assigned to being my second-line supervisor and my former coworker, Ms. Anderson became my first-line supervisor because of that restructuring. The fire was then on the horizon and it was the dawn of Haelee and my troubles.

CHAPTER 2: The Fire

Ms. Anderson and I had a decent relationship prior to the reorganization. Something was different about her after it. She and Ms. Riley, the CoS at the time devised a plan to prove Mr. McDonald as incompetent and incapable of holding his position. They kept a low profile with respect to their scheme however as few people were aware of their insidious plot including myself. I cannot speak in specific terms as to why that was the case, but I do have my ideas as to why it was so. At any rate, they were successful in their efforts to usurp power and control away from him. Mr. McDonald resultantly had to find another job within or outside the Agency or he would be unemployed in the first quarter of 2014. That was most concerning to him because he was the sole financial provider for his family. Notwithstanding he was blessed to find another job within the Agency during the late summer of that year hence a crisis was averted for he and his family. Ms. Riley became my second-line supervisor after Mr. McDonald's departure.

Moving along, I had a meeting with Ms. Riley, Ms. Anderson, and Ms. Evans regarding our program offices strategic posture after she took over command. Ms. Riley asked me to complete a task that was illegal and unethical, per federal regulations during that meeting. I refused to honor her request as it would have placed my career in jeopardy were an audit to occur. Ms. Riley responded by praising me for my knowledge. Her praise was fictitious, however as you will soon learn.

Ms. Riley and Ms. Anderson worked in concert to turn what was once a harmonious environment into one that was entirely toxic for me thereafter. Ms. Anderson reduced my workload and started reassigning my duties to others. The irony was that those others were [admittedly] unqualified and inexperienced in performing those duties. They would resultantly request my assistance in completing those new assignments. I believed that we were all a team; hence I honored their requests for aid where and when needed.

Strike 1

Ms. Anderson stopped including me in meetings. She also revoked my access to the program offices electronic calendars thereby preventing me from being adequately informed about program initiatives, strategies, and results. She also started having me to attend impromptu program review sessions with product owners and project stakeholders with as little as 15 minutes to prepare. I offered no opposition to her requests, and I attended them as requested. Notwithstanding, I would sit anxiously in the meetings, hoping that no one would call on me due to my lack of knowledge on specified topics. I unfortunately could not escape the call to the stage because we were a high priority program office. I would beat around the bush when called upon and speak on whatever I knew. Whether it was old information or not, it was far from me to give direct information. I perceived that Ms. Riley and Ms. Anderson were trying to prove me to be too incompetent to hold my position. I pondered if that was the same thing that they did to Mr. McDonald to usurp his power and have him reassigned.

Moving forward, Ms. Anderson decided that it was appropriate to place me on leave restriction on

13

April 28, 2014. She implied that my use of leave on three different dates during a 14-day period was suspicious. Her reasoning was as follows:

1. On Thursday, April 14, 2014, you called in sick.

2. On Wednesday, April 23, 2014, you arrived at the office and asked to take sick leave at approximately 9:00 AM.

3. You contacted me the next day to report that you were "sick and not well."

4. Your need for leave was questionable in that you were sick on days that you had deadlines or scheduled meetings with your supervisor.

The leave restriction stipulated:

1. Annual leave must be approved at least two days in advance.

2. Circumstances beyond my control should be directly reported to Ms. Anderson between the hours of 7:30 and 8:30 AM. I must provide an estimated duration of any intended absences. No one was authorized to call on my behalf and I had to call daily for the period of my absence under the same parameters.

3. All telework privileges were suspended.

See Appendix 1 for a redacted copy of this letter. While not explicitly stated within, Ms. Anderson marked me as Absent Without Leave (AWOL) if I stayed in the bathroom a little longer than she wanted. AWOL is defined as, "often absent without notice or permission." (Merriam-Webster.com Dictionary). She also marked me as AWOL if I returned to the office or back from lunch three minutes late. I reported for duty at 7:30 AM, and Ms. Anderson at 8:00 AM. I found out from co-workers that she asked them to keep a log of my arrival and departure times and whenever I got up from my desk. Ironically, I had over 400 hours of available and unused annual and sick leave at the time that she placed me on leave restriction.

Humiliation, harassment, and intrusion were the order of the day. Remarkably, no one else on the team seemed to receive an ounce of the mistreatment I received. I was fed up, so I filed a grievance with the American Federation for Government Employees (AFGE) and a discrimination complaint with the Agency's Equal Employment Opportunity (EEO) Office. The intake session allowed me an opportunity to address my high-level concerns and learn about the complaint process. I was relieved when I received word that the EEO Office accepted my complaint and that retaliation was strictly prohibited. It did not matter though because Ms. Anderson began to retaliate by giving me tasks with unrealistic deadlines after finding out about my complaints. To be specific, she would ask me to complete order modifications within an hour, knowing that it historically took a few days to complete them. She would even go to the extent of inquiring how long it would take me to perform specific tasks only to demand that I complete them much sooner than the time frame that I had just communicated to her.

The heat was starting to intensify. I could resultantly see the writing on the wall in that my career with the CoS Office was nearing its conclusion. I resultantly began to seek jobs within and outside of the Agency. I believe that Ms. Anderson might have caught wind of my search because she and Ms. Riley asked me to meet with them to discuss matters as the EEO investigation progressed. I agreed and met with them as requested. To my dismay, Ms. Riley presented me with an offer of a 120-day rotation within a job that I had previously applied for as a full-time employee within the Agency. I pondered how they could have known about my application for the position because the vacancy was still open.

To make matters worse, they informed me that they had set up an interview with the hiring manager for me. I perceived it as part of an elaborate setup. Nonetheless, I participated in the interview, despite my doubts, and it went well. Ms. Anderson informed me that she and Ms. Riley had met with the hiring manager immediately following my interview and that they would be backfilling my position once I accepted the offer for the rotational assignment. I lost interest in the job due to that, and I respectfully declined. I did so because I stood at risk of losing my job, supposing the receiving division was dissatisfied with my performance or lacked the funding for my continued employment. That was a chance that I could not take considering my responsibilities as a single parent. I preferred to either find a permanent full-time position within or outside the Agency. Doing so would afford me the stability that both Haelee and I needed and deserved. I spoke with other Program Directors and Product Owners about joining their teams. They responded that my reputation preceded me and that they would love to have me join

16

their teams. Ms. Riley blocked those efforts in various ways, however.

Strike 2

Ms. Anderson made a point to either be absent or tardy whenever I facilitated meetings. With respect towards her tardiness, she would assert that she showed up late because I did not invite her, and she only found out about the meetings after checking my personal electronic calendar. I had proof that I had indeed invited her to the meetings, but Ms. Anderson would object and infer that I was lying. In addition to her late attendance, she would criticize me when I started meetings without her. She would accuse me of being insubordinate for having done so while simultaneously questioning my competence. She even made a joke about my suffering from amblyopia during a meeting with customers. Amblyopia is defined as, "reduced vision in one eye caused by abnormal visual development early in life." (Lazy eye). I developed a lazy eye due to infant seizures. Those seizures weakened my retina, and it causes my right eye to wander outward. I was taken aback by her joke because no one had done anything of the sort since childhood. Here are the facts: I did invite her to meetings and the invitations were on her calendar; She more than likely removed herself from them out of spite towards me.

Moving forward, I felt a throbbing pain in my back while talking to Ms. Evans on the morning of May 15, 2014. It was as if I were stabbed repeatedly by an invisible dagger. My lungs read the signal for doom, wheezing and gasping were my only defense. My world spun out of control as the pain from the dagger

17

transcended throughout my body. The clouds of doom began to close in on me as I washed away with sweat. The floor became my companion as I met it face first. Ms. Evans helped me up and escorted me to the Agency's Medical Center. If I had never had a near death experience before, this was it. I wished that I woke up in a new Bugatti, but I woke up in the arms of a friend and I was thankful that I survived. I was relieved to find out that I did not have a heart attack. I instead had a panic attack, and it was caused by excessive worry about my career and my ability to provide for Haelee as a single parent.

The attending physician-prescribed medication and directed me to follow up with my primary care physician (PCP) and urged me to use the Agency's Employee Assistance Program (EAP). I followed up with my PCP, as suggested on May 19, 2014. Frequent and sudden periods of intense fear became the order of my days after that initial episode. Insomnia, muscle tension, difficulty concentrating, and increased irritability were comrades who began to know me best. My PCP subsequently referred me to a therapist, Dr. Holtz for additional treatment while simultaneously suggesting that I take leave under the Family Medical Leave Act (FMLA) to rest and consider a change in careers. I took the next few days off following my appointment with Dr. Holtz. I pondered on what my PCP said and agreed that I needed to take extended medical leave. I followed up with my PCP and gave him the WH-380-E Form (Serious Health Condition of Federal Employee) to facilitate extended medical leave.

Strike 3

I returned to duty on May 27, 2014 to find that Ms. Anderson had marked me as AWOL for reporting to work at 7:37 AM on May 16, 2014. Ms. Anderson reduced my timecard by a total of 3 hours and 15 minutes. Her actions were in direct violation of the Agency's Leave Administration Policy, as she did not allow me due process rights. Ms. Anderson failed to note that I had stayed over 30 minutes to make up the 7 minutes of lost time. She also stated that my doctor's notes for the previous week were insufficient.

Her actions were intimidating, revolting, and hurtful. I decided that I would no longer tolerate her unprofessional conduct, so I served her with a Cease-and-Desist Memorandum on May 30, 2014. The memorandum put her on record for retaliation, harassment, and violation of The Notification and Federal Employee Antidiscrimination and Retaliation Act (No FEAR Act). The No FEAR Act, "imposes additional duties upon Federal agency employers intended to reinvigorate their longstanding obligation to provide a work environment free of discrimination and retaliation." (*Questions and Answers*: No FEAR Act). You will find a redacted copy of the memo in Appendix 2.

I made several failed attempts to address the salary discrepancies with payroll but to no avail. While it hurt me financially, I did not belabor the point because Ms. Anderson's harassment came to a halt following receipt of my memorandum. What's more I assumed that everything would work out in time regarding my lost wages particularly as my complaint progressed.

Ms. Anderson started asking my colleagues to deliver messages to me if she had anything to say to me. The only direct communication I received from her were disapproving glances and stares. That suited me fine because she had finally left me alone. I also found it quite amusing and a sense of peace returned to me as a result. By then, my PCP had submitted the WH-380-E form to the Agency's Human Resources Department, and I was waiting for them to process it so that I could get the break that I needed.

Moving along, Ms. Anderson called me into her office for a meeting on June 30, 2014. She and a representative from Human Resources were already there. They asked me to sit down, and they handed me a document. They proposed to suspend me from duty for 30 days without pay within the document under the [false] pretenses of "Conduct Unbecoming," "Failure to Follow Instructions," and "AWOL." They asked me to sign the document and I refused. It was so clear that Ms. Anderson's actions were retaliatory. I was infuriated and panic-stricken at the same time. I stood up so that I could go get the files from my desk and argue that point. I was unable to do so because I soon found myself in one of the most traumatic experiences of my life. I suddenly began to tremble and stutter. Not only that, but my entire body locked up on me. I began to cry as I realized that I could not move or speak. Everything went black thereafter.

CHAPTER 3: Broken to be Blessed

"Dear friends, do not be surprised at the fiery ordeal that has come on you to test you, as though something strange were happening to you. But rejoice inasmuch as you participate in sufferings of Christ, so that you may be overjoyed when his glory is revealed." (*The Holy Bible*, 1 Peter 4:12-13, NIV).

The months and weeks of torment had finally gotten to be too much for me. I resultantly passed out. An eyewitness said that my eyes rolled back in my head, I fell backwards in the space between Ms. Anderson's office and the work floor, and that I had a seizure. Someone contacted the Agency's onsite emergency personnel and 911. Another witness told me that the emergency personnel asked, "what did y'all do to him" as they administered treatment. There were no answers of course. At any rate, the paramedics rolled me on my side, checked my oxygen levels, checked my blood pressure, and administered oxygen. They placed me on a stretcher once they determined that it was safe to move me and rushed me to the closest emergency room. Eyewitnesses told me that Ms. Anderson had a smile on her face throughout the ordeal.

A senior co-worker, Mr. Simmons, came by the emergency room to inform me that he was unsure about what had occurred while expressing sympathies. He said that while he was sympathetic to my plight, he was not there for that reason. He informed me that the Agency's policy stipulated that either my supervisor, Ms. Anderson, or my manager, Ms. Riley, were supposed to accompany me to the emergency room until they contacted my family or until I was released [whichever came first]. He also told me that they had been arguing about who should go check on me. Neither one of them wanted to do so hence they sent him as their proxy to check on me and report back to them on my wellbeing.

The physicians put me through a medley of neurological assessments to determine what was going on with me while Mr. Simmons waited. They concluded that I had experienced a panic attack and a nervous breakdown. Have you ever been so emotionally and physically overwhelmed by life's demands that you were temporarily unable to function? If your answer is "yes," then I understand because that is exactly what happened to me. While the physicians were concerned, they did not believe that my condition was extreme enough to admit me for inpatient treatment. They resultantly decided that they would release me to my recognizance so long as Mr. Simmons or someone else could give me a ride home and watch over me. While Mr. Simmons was happy that I was okay, he was unable to take me home because he had a family commitment to attend to. He also informed me that he would not share my condition with either Ms. Anderson or Ms. Riley. I thanked him and told him that I understood as he departed. I called Ms. Evans and asked her if she could pick me up from the hospital and take me home. The irony was that she was at another hospital with her then-boyfriend, now her husband. He was undergoing a surgical procedure, and she was waiting for him to wake up. I told her that I understood and that I would find some other way home and we hung up. She called back shortly thereafter and asked me which hospital I was at. I told her where I was, and she responded that she was on

23

her way to pick me up and take me home. I told her that it was okay and that she was where she needed to be and should have been. She said, "boy you're family. I'm on my way like I said." She picked me up, drove me home, helped me into my house, helped me get comfortable, and told me that she and Ms. Taylor would come by the following day to check on me and bring me my car and belongings.

Ms. Evans and Ms. Taylor came by the next morning as Ms. Evans promised. They returned my belongings, cooked breakfast for me, and tried to get me to laugh and talk. They were unsuccessful in their attempts to make me laugh, but they did get me to talk a little. They were astounded to find out that I suddenly developed a speech impediment. That was most concerning to them because I never had one before. They had to get back to work so they could not stay long. They hugged me, said their goodbyes, and promised that they would be checking on me. I laid down and took a nap after they left. I was later awakened by an unexpected call from Ms. Riley. I did not want to speak to her, so I let the call go to voicemail. She left a message saying, "Hi Dedrick this is Ms. Riley. I was just calling to check on you to see how things are going. If you're feeling well enough, please give me a call back. I hope that all else is good. Bye." I did not return her call because I knew it to be insincere. What's more, I was sickened by the sound of her voice. Notwithstanding, I still have that message saved on my voicemail today. I cannot tell you why I have kept it. I can only say that I cannot bring myself to delete it for some reason.

Moving forward, I was extremely irritated, depressed, anxious, and embarrassed by my speech impediment. I did not know who to trust, and I did not want to talk about my ordeal. I subsequently isolated myself from Ms. Evans, Ms. Taylor, and everyone close to me except for my mom and Haelee. There was no way that I could return to work in the condition that I was in. I resultantly took extended medical leave under the provisions of FMLA. I confessed to my mom that I could no longer take care of Haelee and that I did not know what to do. I hated to admit it, but I had to be honest for both my and Haelee's sake. I felt like a complete failure at that point and it hurt as I cried into the phone. My mom told me that I needed to focus on myself in the interim and she offered to take care of Haelee until I was healthy enough to do so again. She assured me that I was not a bad parent and that I would be back to my old self in due time. I accepted my mom's offer and sent Haelee to spend the summer with her in North Carolina as she suggested.

I spent the next several weeks doing nothing more than resting, reading, and attending therapy. Dr. Holtz informed me that I had developed agoraphobia in addition to my previously diagnosed anxiety and panic disorders. Agoraphobia is someone who has an intense fear of public transportation, being in open spaces, being outside their homes, being in crowds, and being in enclosed spaces. Individuals who suffer from it typically display at least two of those symptoms. At any rate, I was sitting alone in my bedroom reading my Bible on June 12, 2014 when I received a phone call out of the blue. The caller, Mrs. Schmidt wanted me to come in for an interview. You will find out more about that in Chapter 4.

CHAPTER 4: Not All Roads Lead to Gold

Mrs. Schmidt was calling in response to a Project Manager position that I had applied for with her Agency. She liked what she saw on my application and resume; hence she wanted to invite me in for an interview. I was ecstatic because I had long been considering career opportunities with her Agency. The Agency had historically been noted as one of the best places to work per the annual Best Places to Work in Government Series and Employment Viewpoint Surveys. Not only that, but the position was a promotion, and it would come with a significant raise. Notwithstanding, I considered declining the offer because I was still recovering from my ordeal. I was concerned about having a panic attack during the interview. After consulting Dr. Holtz, we agreed that I would not have much to lose in at least trying. I subsequently accepted Mrs. Schmidt's offer for an interview on June 16, 2014, at 10:30 AM by faith.

The agency was approximately a 1 hour and 45-minute ride away from my house in Maryland. With that in mind, I would need to leave the house around 8:45 AM to arrive on time. I decided to leave the house at 7:00 AM instead. I arrived at the interview location in Washington, DC around 9:00 AM. That suited me fine because doing so afforded me an opportunity to better prepare in surveying the landscape, gathering my emotions, and praying. My prayer was centered around a scripture that reads, "Do not say, 'I am too young.' You must go to everyone I send you to and say whatever I command you. Do not be afraid of them, for I am with you and will rescue you," declares the Lord. Then the Lord reached out his hand and touched my mouth and said to me, "I have put my words in your mouth. See, today I appoint you over nations and kingdoms to uproot and tear down, to destroy and overthrow, to build and to plant." (*The Holy Bible*, Jeremiah 1:7 - 10). I prayed that He would do for me as He did for Jeremiah on that very day.

Mrs. Schmidt came downstairs to greet me at 10:15 AM and she escorted me to the conference room. Mrs. Stance and Mr. Berry were already seated in the room in preparation for the interview. It was a scenario-based panel interview wherein they each took turns asking me a series of questions. I took slow shallow breaths before answering each question to keep myself from becoming nervous and stuttering. I felt optimistic after completing the interview because Mrs. Schmidt smiled throughout it. I returned home with a smile and a prayer of gratitude on my heart because I knew that nobody could have afforded me the opportunity but God. I promptly prepared thank you letters for each member of the interview panel and I sent them over via email.

Moving along, I received a tentative offer of employment from the Agency on July 2, 2014, and I promptly accepted it. Doing so afforded me a release from the months of harassment, discrimination, and agitation that I had endured at the other Agency. One issue was that my medical team had not yet cleared me to return to duty for either my current employer or any other one for that matter as I was still recovering. My medical team had me undergo a barrage of tests to determine my readiness and prepare me for a return to duty. I could not return to my former Agency because of the damage that had been done.

29

Dr. Holtz determined that I was well enough to report to duty with the new Agency effective July 27, 2014. I happily submitted a letter of resignation to my former Agency, picked up my belongings, and completed exit counseling. I was elated to find out that neither Ms. Riley nor Ms. Anderson placed false claims within my personnel file. Not only that, but they both decided to take leave on the day that I went to pick up my belongings. I never heard from either one of them again thereafter. I for one could not have been any happier because God had given me a fresh start and I was eagerly looking forward to it.

July 27, 2014, finally came, and my fresh start began. I completed orientation, received my IT equipment, toured the facility, met my new co-workers, and received an overview of operations and our strategic initiatives. I was responsible for analyzing and determining the impact that new regulations, executive orders, and directives would have on the government enterprise while working with external federal agencies to implement them within this new position. All was well, and Mrs. Schmidt and I were accomplishing wonderful things within and across the enterprise as 2014 came to an end.

I unfortunately became more anxious as time went on due to the extended commute from Maryland to Washington, DC. My commute went from being 15 – 20 minutes at my previous Agency to 1 hour and 45-minutes as previously disclosed. But not only that there were constant breakdowns on the subway in addition to an adjustment of being in the office five days per week under those conditions. I did everything within my power to suppress my anxieties, but I ultimately failed. I subsequently had a panic attack at work on September 15, 2015. Mrs. Schmidt escorted me to the Agency's Medical Center for treatment. I shared with the attending physician that I had agoraphobia, panic disorder, and anxiety disorder. I was once again prescribed rest as they administered medication and secured a cab to take me home. Before releasing me, they suggested that I start thinking about an emergency management plan and reasonable accommodations. They offered to aid in the development of those plans if I needed assistance. I accepted their offer to develop a plan in coordination with Mrs. Schmidt and my medical team. We worked together to establish a set of reasonable accommodations that worked best for the business unit and myself. The agreement was that I would need to report to the office for at most 4 hours per day, and the remaining 4 hours could be completed from home. That allowed me to avoid heavy traffic and crowds of people in the mornings and afternoons while commuting to and from work.

Things did not work out as we hoped because I was continuously hampered and limited by my condition. I subsequently went back to Mrs. Schmidt and inquired about a switch to 100% telework in January 2016. As per her response, "a project manager must interact with other external agencies and must travel locally so that's not going to work." She wanted to help me but needed time to think things through. Mrs. Schmidt got back with me a few days later and asked me about my knowledge of acquisitions and contracts. I informed her that I was extremely familiar with that line of work and she retorted that she had found something that might work out for me. She told me that the Project Management Office (PMO) needed a full-time Contract Specialist and that the position supported virtual work. She stated that the position was mine if I wanted it but that I would need to accept a transfer and submit a request for 100% telework to the Director of the PMO, Ms. Rain, who would be my new first-line supervisor. I was delighted because I knew that it was the big break that I needed professionally. It unfortunately was not a break personally as you will learn in the chapters to follow.

CHAPTER 5: The Bully

I jumped ahead a little in the previous chapter, where I shared my need for reasonable accommodations. Doing so left out some critical and disturbing personal events. Some of those events were shared in The Rules of a Big Boss: A book of self-love, where the author, Haelee [my daughter and co-author] discussed being bullied from her perspective. I will take a deeper dive into things in sharing them from my perspective in this and subsequent chapters.

Haelee shared that she had a play date with one of her classmates at their house. We will call this classmate Anonymous to maintain consistency with the nomenclature from The Rules of a Big Boss: A book of self-love. At any rate, Anonymous pinned her up against wall while they were playing and attempted to kiss her. Haelee went on to say that she tried to escape by turning her head, covering her mouth, and saying, "no." Anonymous persisted by attempting to place her hands down my daughters pants to stimulate her private parts. Haelee shoved her away, left the room, requested to call me, and asked me to come pick her up. She did not immediately share what transpired; she only shared that she no longer wanted to play with Anonymous going forward. I explained that she did not have to play with anyone that she did not want to but that it would be difficult to achieve, given that they shared several of the same friends. I told her that she could play by herself or with another friend to avoid her in the future if she wanted. I still had no clue what had happened, however.

I noticed a change in my daughter in the days thereafter because she had been distant and reserved. I knew that something was wrong, but I could not ascertain what was going on nor could I get her to share. I asked her repeatedly over the next several weeks what was bothering her only for her to respond, "nothing, I'm okay Daddy." I assumed that she might have been experiencing growing pains, so I left it alone.

Haelee started avoiding Anonymous in February 2015 and she did not take a liking to it. Anonymous responded by bullying her incessantly. One of those incidents occurred on March 14, 2015 where Anonymous coaxed my daughter into playing rock, paper, scissors with her. Haelee assumed that things would be okay because their mutual friends were playing too, but boy was she wrong. Anonymous got upset because Haelee kept winning and she retorted by strangling her. The other children had to remove Anonymous' hands from around her neck so that she could breathe. Another event transpired on April 25, 2015, where Anonymous caressed Haelee's butt and attempted to kiss her during the school's aftercare program. Haelee did not immediately share what occurred when I arrived to pick her up. She waited until we got home instead. I was mortified by what she shared with me and that she did not consult me sooner. Her failure to tell me when I initially picked her up robbed me of the opportunity to immediately address matters with the aftercare and school personnel. Notwithstanding, I reached out to the offender's mom, Mrs. Anonymous to make her aware of what was happening in hopes that we might be able to alleviate matters. I assumed that we could have a fruitful conversation because she and I were friendly at the time. She unfortunately did not take kindly to my accusations. She responded by accusing Haelee of assaulting and harassing her daughter instead. I was stunned and angered by her incredulous reaction. I remained calm however and simply told her to keep Anonymous away from my daughter while promising that I would do the same. I notified the school administrators the next day of what had transpired. They said they did not have much control over what occurred after school hours because they did not manage the aftercare program. They did say that they would pass my concerns over to the appropriate officials within the program. I did not have much faith that they would hence I reached out to the program officials myself. They advised me that they would investigate my claims and be more mindful of things going forward.

Things were going well following my outreach, or so I thought that is until May 25, 2015 because Anonymous struck again. She attempted to drown Haelee in our neighborhood pool by forcefully submerging her head under the water knowing that Haelee could not swim. One of Haelee's friends rescued her by pulling Anonymous off her and helping her out of the water. Haelee and her friends ran to my house and told me what had happened. Her mom, Ms. Baltimore was visiting with us on that day and I told her that she needed to speak with Mrs. Anonymous about her daughter's behavior. Ms. Baltimore did that very thing. Mrs. Anonymous was apologetic and said that she would talk to her daughter about matters as requested.

Anonymous Pulled a Fast One

Another incident transpired on July 12, 2015 where Anonymous apologized to Haelee and promised to stop harassing her. Haelee accepted her apology, and they agreed to hug it out. Haelee let her defenses down, and Anonymous took advantage of that by lifting her off the ground and bear hugging her to squeeze the life out of her. Thank God for sensible eyewitnesses because they pried her arms from around Haelee and separated them before she passed out or worst yet died. Haelee ran home and shared what had occurred with me.

I sought counsel from my mom, given that she had/has been a Licensed Clinical Social Worker (LCSW) for over 30 years. Anonymous was 6 years old and Haelee was 7 at the time so it was a Juvenile Services issue according to my mom. My mom stated that Juvenile Services would not intervene in a case such as this due to the age of the offender and a lack of specialized resources. I told Ms. Baltimore that she needed to speak with Mrs. Anonymous again and she did. Mrs. Anonymous apologized, promised that she would talk to her daughter and that further offenses would cease. Ms. Baltimore accepted her apology and we assumed that all was well. Notwithstanding I took the initiative to contact the Police Department, Social Services, and our community association about matters. The Police Department and Social Services took initial intake reports, but I did not receive any additional correspondence from them after that. Our community manager was empathetic, but she was unsure of what she could do besides remain vigilant.

Daddy Takes the Lead

I believe in being proactive, not reactive; hence, I decided that Haelee and I would have a family meeting with the school administrators once school started back. Haelee and I shared what transpired between her and Anonymous at the conclusion of the previous school year and over the summer. The school administrators assured us that Haelee could come to them with any concerns that she had. They also claimed that they would investigate matters and keep things under control. That promise was short-lived however because Anonymous continued to assault Haelee. She also started spreading sexually perverted rumors about her at school. Haelee told me that the school administrators acted like they did not believe her when she confided in them. She said that they acted like things were all in her imagination. That negatively impacted her trust in them to the point that despondence and depression set in. That distrust led to the development of school phobia within her.

Things got worse during the Labor Day weekend of 2015. I was indoors preparing food with our then next-door neighbor and friend, Ms. Glenn. Haelee kept a short distance away from me while the other children were outside playing. Ms. Glenn told Haelee that she should be outside playing with the other children instead of being inside with us. I agreed with her and encouraged Haelee to go outside and play with her friends. That was a mistake because Anonymous came outdoors not too long afterward. Anonymous and Haelee got into an argument and she responded by punching Haelee in the stomach. Haelee collapsed to the ground, gasping, and struggling for air. Anonymous continued her assault by kicking and stomping on Haelee as she laid prone on the ground. Haelee returned to the house with a limp but she would not divulge what happened to her. She only said that she was tired of playing and that she simply wanted to eat and watch TV. I did not persist in asking her what transpired because I knew that she would tell me eventually.

Moving along, Haelee shared with me that she had been in a fight with Anonymous once we returned home that evening. But not only that, Haelee also divulged that her friends told her not to tell me what happened out of fear that I would be angry. To make matters worse, she shared with me that her friends recorded the entire thing but deleted it. I was outraged and devastated following her reveal. I consulted my mom considering her previously mentioned expertise. She responded that there was no standard approach for matters of the sort. With that in mind she said that Haelee would have to fight back if Anonymous continued to put her hands on her. I held Haelee in my arms that evening, and I cried in despair as she drifted off to sleep, but my anxiety did not allow me to sleep. I believed that I failed her as a parent because I did not teach her how to defend herself, and I agreed to let her play outside.

Pause and Reflect

We sometimes miss critical steps in our parenting journey because we believe that our children will be safe so long as they are well mannered but boy was I wrong. It is okay though because I am far from

39

perfect. What's more parenting does not come with a handbook, so I was bound to make mistakes as are you. The key is that we acknowledge our respective mistakes and take the lessons needed from them.

Enough!

I sent Haelee to the car to grab something for me that following afternoon. She did not return in a reasonable time frame, so I went to check on her. She was frozen with fear because Anonymous was sitting on our front steps. I told her, "ignore her, walk past her, and fight back if she puts her hands on you" and I went back inside. Haelee said, "okay," and she went to retrieve the item. Anonymous forcefully shoved her against the railing of our steps as she attempted to walk past her and back into the house. Haelee told me that she hurt her ribs because of that attack. I told her that she needed to go back outside and defend herself; otherwise, things would continue to get worse. Haelee shared that she was afraid of getting beat up again. She also expressed grace and humility in not wanting to fight Anonymous because she was much larger than her and that she did not want to hurt her. I assured her that it would not happen again, and that I would be there to support her.

We soon exited our home to find Anonymous still sitting on our steps. She smiled as we exited and held her middle fingers up at us both. I ran out of tolerance for the nonsense, so it was about to go down. I told the other children to hurry home while simultaneously telling Haelee to fight her. Haelee responded by launching fists of furry all over Anonymous. She was literally whooping her like she

40

stole something. Anonymous pleaded for mercy with each punch but Haelee would not relent. She literally beat her like she stole something, and she did. While I was amused by seeing Haelee get her revenge, I called her off but not before telling her to pick Anonymous up and toss her in the bushes. If proud were a person, it had to have been me at that very moment. I responded by telling Haelee that I was proud of her while giving her a high five and a hug. Our glee did not last long however because there was a knock at our door that evening, and the Sherriff was standing on the other side. You will find out more about that turn of events in Chapter 6.

CHAPTER 6: Surprise, Surprise

Haelee and I were eating dinner when we heard a knock at the door. I looked out the peep hole and saw The Sherriff standing on the other side. He said that he had previously taken statements from the Anonymous family and our next-door neighbor about the events that transpired earlier as I opened the door. He then wanted to take a statement from me. I invited him in, grabbed my laptop, and showed him a spreadsheet that outlined the litany of harassment and abuse that Haelee had undergone at the hands of Anonymous. I let him know that we were fed up with her shenanigans and toxic behaviors, so we took action. The Sheriff was empathetic and inquired about the steps we took to alleviate the pain. I retorted that I had previously contacted the Police Department and Social Services about matters but that no action had been taken regarding matters to my knowledge. He said that it was good that I had done that, but that the advice that my mom gave was partially correct. He inferred that I should have contacted Juvenile Services myself for intake and investigation. He also stated that the school should have contacted Juvenile Services because they are/were mandatory reporters. He asked if I could give him a copy of the spreadsheet that I had been keeping so as he could enter it with the report. I said that I could, and happily provided a copy as requested. He also recommended that I go down to the Magistrate's Office to file a complaint and request a peace order against the Anonymous family.

I took the Sherriff's advice and did that very thing on the morning of September 9, 2015 after dropping Haelee off at school. As [bad] luck may have it, Anonymous' parents were already at the Magistrates Office. I hoped that we would be able to keep things civil, but they would not allow it. They rushed out of the office as soon as they saw me approaching, and a fight ensued between Mr. Anonymous and I while Mrs. Anonymous cheered the struggle. The police came out and ordered the Anonymous' back inside to finish their statement while I waited outside. I would be allowed to enter once they were finished to give my own statement. I provided a synopsis of events that had transpired over the past several months on entering and requested a protective order be entered to keep the Anonymous' away from Haelee. The magistrate approved my request after hearing the sordid history and she granted an initial peace order for six months. I took the peace order to Haelee's school and community association immediately thereafter. I felt a sense of relief as I returned home as I believed that things were finally over. That sense of relief did not last long however because I found a criminal summons attached to my door. I opened it up to find out that I was being charged with Second Degree Assault on a Minor. That crime is/was punishable by up to 10 years in prison, a $2,500 in fine, or both if found guilty. I was completely dismayed and crestfallen. How on earth did I become the villain for simply instructing Haelee to defend herself? I literally could not believe what my eyes were seeing. I did not spend much time thinking about things because I knew that I needed to get an attorney and fast.

I could not afford to take any chances with this case hence I hopped on every legal marketplace to locate the best criminal defense attorney. I decided to procure the representation of the most high-profile attorney in the state after holding a few consultations with others. At issue was that it would cost me $10,000 for his representation and I only had $6,000 in savings at the time. I would have had so much more had my previous employer not repeatedly allowed Ms. Anderson to place me in an AWOL status or paid me back for my lost wages. I did not dwell on that, however. I simply reached out to my mom for a gift to help cover my legal fees. I also set up a GoFundMe to help me raise funds.

I was blessed enough to secure the necessary funds for my legal defense, but my attorney decided to move the goal post by increasing the fees to **$20,000**. I asked him how on Earth did he expect me to come up with $20,000 when I had trouble coming up with $10,000? I also asked where was the logic in his doing so? He explained that the case was more complicated than he initially thought, and as such, he had to charge accordingly. I called my mom, and she withdrew money from her retirement account to help me cover my legal fees. I then had the funds that I needed to secure my legal defense or so I thought.

My attorney came back and requested an additional **$7,500** in funding, following a pre-trial hearing on December 15, 2015. To be clear, the cost of my defense had now gone from $10,000 to **$27,500**. He stated that the starting price for most of his cases is/was $30,000 and that he was doing me a favor by taking on my case at a lower fee. What's more, he stated that he was not the one who told Haelee to go out and break the law, and I was within my rights to

45

find a new attorney. I was devastated by his indifference.

His partner reached out to me not too long after that meeting. He said that he overhead my conversation with his partner and that he was disturbed by it. He stated that it was not the first time that he had seen his partner mistreat a client and that he did not approve of it. He offered to represent me, not as a member of the firm, but as independent counsel. I thanked him and agreed to his representation. He followed up by filing a change of legal counsel proposition with the court. He proffered that it would have been an open-and-shut case had things happened in an urban community. It unfortunately happened in an extremely suburban community. On that note, he stated that the prosecutor, Mr. Jones wanted to elevate his profile by bringing down a high-ranking government employee. He also inferred that race played a factor in things as well and that he was disappointed by it all. Notwithstanding he assured me that he would devise strategies to win the case so that Haelee and I could get the justice we deserved.

January 5, 2016 arrived, and it was time for opening arguments and the trial. My attorney began by conveying that the case was more complicated than what was presented by Mr. Jones. He shared how Anonymous had long been Haelee's tormentor and that it had significant effects on her from a psychological and emotional perspective. He also shared how the school administration failed us in both not making the appropriate contacts to Juveniles Services or instructing me to do so amongst other things.

Mr. Jones opened his case by accusing Haelee of assaulting Anonymous unprovoked and bullying her. He provided evidence that included photos of abrasions and medical bills. Anonymous and her parents taunted Haelee and I throughout the trial. I believe that they might have forgotten that it was being recorded. The false accusations and taunting had Haelee in tears. My attorney's paralegal consoled her the best that she could and assured her that justice would be served, and that the truth would prevail in the end.

My attorney used the documentation that I had compiled to show that Anonymous had long been bullying Haelee thereby calling her and her parents' credibility into question. Mr. Jones realized that neither Haelee nor I were the villains but victims as the trial continued. He resultantly offered my attorney a settlement where he allowed me to plead "Not Guilty" as opposed to "Guilty" in response to all charges. He also waived the civil penalties and the request for medical payments. I was still guilty of a crime despite his allowing me to plead "Not Guilty." He resultantly proposed an atonement of my spending six months on unsupervised probation, 48 hours in a minimum-security prison, payment of court fees, and 12 weeks of anger management counseling in exchange for him dropping all charges against me. The Anonymous family was enraged because they wanted me to receive the maximum penalty allowable under the law. Haelee and I were ecstatic because God had shown up and showed out late in the midnight hour as He had for Paul and Silas [in the Bible]. The specific scripture reads as, "About midnight Paul and Silas were praying and singing hymns to God, and the other prisoners were listening to them. Suddenly there was such a violent earthquake that the foundations of the prison were shaken. At once all the prison doors flew open, and everyone's chains came loose." (*The Holy Bible*, Acts 16:25 - 26). To God be the Glory.

CHAPTER 7: The Transfer

As a fair warning, this chapter is a new level. You may want to hold onto your seatbelts because President Obama got involved.

I sent letters via email to the Superintendent of Schools, Ombudsmen, Board of Education, and County Delegates on December 7, 2015. I wanted to make them aware of the excessive bullying and the school administration's negligence. I resultantly wanted to request an out of district transfer to another school for Haelee. Anonymous' behavior became more unacceptable by the day, and it was too painful to bear. Given that sentiment, I believed that Haelee would be best served in a fresh environment. You will find a redacted copy of that letter in Appendix 3.

The Administrative Director requested to meet with me following receipt of my email. We discussed my concerns regarding bullying, harassment, intimidation, sexual assault, and suitable corrective actions among other things on December 8, 2015. He agreed that an out of district transfer would be most appropriate for my daughter. Notwithstanding he was not the decision authority on such matters, so he forwarded my query to the School Reassignment Office and pressed upon them the criticality of my request in hopes of influencing them to approve it. He assured me that he would follow up with the school administrators. While I had my doubts that a conversation with them would be worthwhile, I agreed to meet with them, nonetheless.

Haelee's school held an assembly for students that made the Honor Roll later that afternoon and I was invited to attend as her special invited guest. I of course accepted as it was an honor to support her in any way that I could [and it still is]. I arrived on campus just before the start of the assembly to sign in, only to be turned away by the Principal. She said that the peace order prohibited my appearance on school grounds, and that I was only allowed to pick up and drop Haelee off at school going forward. I asked was there any way that they could call her to the office so that I could congratulate her and let her know that I would not be able to attend but the principal said, "no." She inferred that it would be a disruptive for either Haelee or Anonymous to see me and she directed me to leave. I disputed her claim, given that I was a member of the PTA and a school volunteer. I also knew that it was nothing but retaliation following my complaints to the Superintendent and others. I did not want to cause a scene, so I did not belabor my points. I simply turned around to leave. The Principal concluded matters by inviting me to meet with her and the Vice Principal via telephone on December 14, 2015, at 9:30 AM before I left. I went home feeling sad and confused and I could not help but cry as my anxiety intensified. I wondered if Haelee would feel further abandoned and what she would think of my not being there. I could not spend too much time feeling sad however because something had to be done and fast. I subsequently pulled myself together and sent yet another letter to the Superintendent to let her know that the Principal had retaliated against Haelee and I because I exercised my right to file a complaint. You will find a redacted copy of that letter in Appendix 4.

Moving along, I received word that our State Delegates would be hosting a Town Hall later that evening. They were doing so because they were concerned about the rise in complaints about the school system. Parents, students, teachers, and community members all had the opportunity to vocalize their issues. The Baltimore Sun and ABC News were set to cover the event. Haelee and I attended and were front and center as the first people to speak. The night's proceedings commenced with her account of the bullying and the sexual assault that she had experienced. I concluded our presentation by sharing the school systems inaction in addressing matters. The audience and other speakers showered Haelee with praise for her courage as we sat down. I assumed that things would be better after that, but that could not have been any further from the truth because there was still no response regarding my request for an out of district transfer to another school.

I decided to escalate matters to the White House, Congress, and the County Executive. I specifically chose to write a letter to President Obama. While it was a complete shot in the dark, I shared what Haelee and I had been going through. I hoped and prayed that he would respond. You will find a copy of that letter in Appendix 5. President Obama surprisingly responded on December 11, 2015. He said in short, "we must ensure young Americans can learn in safe environments and can find and receive help from caring adults. To learn more about my Administration's commitment to addressing bullying and finding resources, please visit www.StopBullying.gov." You will find a copy of that letter in Appendix 6. President

Obama also forwarded my letter to the Office of Civil Rights (OCR) with the US Department of Education for investigation. A representative sent me a note on January 5, 2016. She explained that the OCR enforces several federal laws and that I had the right to file an official complaint. You will find a copy of that letter in Appendix 7.

The US Department of Education accepted my complaint and launched an investigation effective January 15, 2016. The school system was resultantly in jeopardy of losing federal funding because of my complaint. The Superintendent decided to approve my request to transfer Haelee thereafter with a simple response of "approved." My daughter became a local celebrity, and her new school welcomed her with open arms. Her new Principal told us quite simply, "we don't play that here," and she meant it. Haelee and I were over the moon as she finally had a fresh start in a healthy learning environment that was conducive towards learning and student safety.

Ignite

Can we pause for a moment and reflect on the goodness of the almighty God? His word says, "When you pass through the waters, I will be with you; and when you pass through the rivers, they will not sweep over you. When you walk through the fire, you will not be burned; the flames will not set you ablaze." (*The Holy Bible*, Isaiah 43:2, NIV).

We often make plans for living life like it's golden only to fall into despair or give up when things get hot. But fire is not always as harmful as we tend to believe. Yes, it burns and yes it can destroy but it also brings forth light. As a reminder, God led the Israelites through the Red Sea using fire to light their way. We must do the same in letting our respective fires lead us to victories just as it did them.

What fiery trials are you going through?

Can you see the light amidst the flames?

The light that you see will keep the flames from harming or consuming you. That light will propel you to victory. The subsequent chapters are where the fire becomes extremely hot but hold on because it all ends in light.

CHAPTER 8: Too Good to be True

I previously mentioned that I would need to undergo a career change to accommodate my disability status and the need for reasonable accommodations. I was ecstatic as I believed it would afford me a much-needed reprieve. I was reassigned to working for Ms. Rain in January 2016 after accepting the change. She stated that she understood that I needed reasonable accommodations and asked me to confirm if it was true. I said that it was, and she instructed me to look over the reasonable accommodation's manual, fill out the request for accommodations form, send it back to her, and that we would work with the Reasonable Accommodations Program Manager, Mrs. Richland, to process my request upon receipt.

I did as Ms. Rain instructed and submitted my request on February 4, 2016. Mrs. Richland followed up by sending me a request for medical information (RMI) on February 16, 2016. She specifically wanted to know the following:

1. Describe and explain the severity, and duration of this person's medical conditions, to include anxiety disorder and panic disorder.

2. What major life activities of this individual are affected by the condition/s?

3. What are the current functional limitations of this person?

4. Please explain how the prescribed medication may impede this person's ability to sustain the capacity to perform work during a full business day.

5. Describe and explain the triggers related to this person's need to commute to work and interact with others in the workplace as it is associated with these conditions.

6. This person reported that he recently had frequent anxiety and panic attacks during business hours, and he is managing symptoms via medication and sleep. Please explain the frequency and duration of this person's episodes.

7. This person reported he suffers from insomnia. Please explain the severity of this condition and how it may impede this person's capacity to sustain the capacity to perform work during a full business day.

8. Please describe this person's current treatment plan and explain the prognosis for improved health.

9. What accommodations may the employer provide to support the employee's challenges while in the work environment?

I gave a copy of the RMI to Dr. Holtz and she was aghast at the sight of it. She retorted that she had never seen a request for such in-depth information for reasonable accommodations in all her years of practice. She had specific concerns with respect to bullets 2, 3, and 4. She stated that the information request was intrusive, and that she could not share that information unless I completed a Health Insurance Portability and Accountability (HIPAA) Release Form. A HIPAA

Release Form protects patients from unauthorized disclosure of their medical records. She advised me not to fill it out because she did not believe that the Agency needed that much information to determine my disability status.

Dr. Holtz also stated that releasing such information could work against me in my future career with the Agency or others hence it would behoove me to keep my health data private. Notwithstanding, she honored their request without my signing a HIPAA Release Form. She was cautious in her response to protect me without violating my rights. She released the requested medical documentation on February 26, 2016. I gave that information to Mrs. Richland the following business day. Mrs. Richland said that the medical documentation was insufficient, and she requested more data. I went back to Dr Holtz with her request and she said that the Agency was putting us in a bind because they were either trying to coerce me into signing a HIPAA Release Form or for her to release my protected health data without it. Dr. Holtz reiterated that it was in my best interest to refrain from signing the form but also that my refusal to do so could jeopardize her licensure. She assured me that she would figure out some type of way to honor the request while simultaneously adhering to federal standards. Dr. Holtz released a second release of [partial] medical data on March 1, 2016. She did so with a warning that she would not do so again unless I signed a HIPAA Release Form. She also stated that she would drop me as a patient if I asked her to participate in the process again without first signing the form. Dr. Holtz also recommended that I hire an attorney that specialized in disabilities and accommodations. I decided against that because I wanted to believe that the Agency was operating in good faith. I ultimately came to regret that decision as you will soon learn.

Moving forward, I handed the updated release of medical documentation to Mrs. Richland on March 2, 2016. Her response was the same as it was the first time, insufficient. She resultantly requested even more data. I explained that Dr. Holtz was not going to provide any additional information regarding my health or disability status unless I signed a HIPAA Release Form. I also informed Mrs. Richland that Dr. Holtz cautioned me not to sign it because it would protect me from malicious actors. What's more, she also said that the information that she previously provided was more than sufficient to determine my need for accommodations. Mrs. Richland said okay, and she asked to meet with Ms. Rain and me to discuss matters in detail immediately thereafter. The three of us met a few weeks later to review the information and discuss my request. Ms. Rain and Mrs. Richland both advised that the information that I provided was insufficient for them, and they requested more data during the meeting. I persisted in reiterating that neither Dr. Holtz nor I would be providing any additional written documentation. They continued to persist despite my repeatedly rebuffing their efforts. I became upset at their continued insistence to the point that I had an anxiety attack. Mrs. Richland resultantly cut the meeting short and I took sick leave for the remainder of the day thereafter.

We met once more on May 12, 2016. Mrs. Richland and Ms. Rain persisted in requesting even more intrusive medical data. I would not relent because we had already given them plenty of medical data. They refused to accept that fact, however. Mrs. Richland finally convinced me by saying that I would not have to provide my medical data again if I provided it to them right there and then. She literally said that she would place it in my Human Resources File such that I would not have to worry about going through the process again in the future. I finally relented in verbally providing the requested data. They thanked me for participating and said that they would take everything under consideration. Ms. Rain finally approved my request for 100% telework on June 14, 2016. She placed a caveat in the written agreement that my request for accommodations may be reviewed after March 31, 2017 if my medical condition changed, to confirm the state of my medical condition, and/or if the essential functions of my job changed. She also said that I had seven days to dispute her decision to my second-line supervisor if I disagreed with her decision. I, of course, did not disagree with any part of the decision. I resultantly went back to Dr. Holtz and let her know that they finally approved my request. She and I celebrated because we knew that it would be therapeutic for Haelee and myself.

CHAPTER 9: The Move

Dr. Holtz understood that Haelee and I had been through an unprecedented degree of trauma. She feared that Haelee would become a target of retaliation by the Anonymous family and the school system given that the latter was under federal investigation. She subsequently recommended that we consider relocating because my mom was/is a LCSW. She also made that recommendation with the understanding that we have family members that work in the school system. As such she believed that Haelee would be better protected and that it would be therapeutic for us both if we considered moving to North Carolina. I was reluctant to make the move because finding a new physician would be a task and Dr. Holtz had seen us through so much. She was empathetic to our plight, so she offered to continue to treat me albeit on a virtual basis and I agreed.

While I loved Dr. Holtz's idea of relocating, I needed to talk things over with my mom to get her approval. My mom agreed that it was a great idea, and she invited us to move in with her for a while. I contacted a few relocation companies and realtors, put our house on the market, and prepared to move. Haelee and I resultantly moved in with my mom in July 2016. I was discouraged about it because I had not lived with her since college. My self-esteem was at an all-time low, but I reminded myself that it was for the best.

We placed all our belongings in storage except for our bedroom furniture and clothing. We set our bedrooms up at my mom's house exactly as they were in our previous locale. We did so because we wanted to have some semblance of familiarity, comfortability, and normalcy.

I began to realize how much my mom needed me and how much we needed her after we moved in. My mom needed me to be closer to home because she could not get around like she used to. A lot of things needed to be repaired around the house and she did not have the skills nor dexterity to perform a lot of do-it-yourself projects. She also did not have the money to perform the projects that required skilled labor after giving and loaning me so much money.

My mom developed a motherly type of relationship with Haelee during that time. She did this by taking her for trips to the salon to get their hair, nails, and feet done together. They would also go out to brunch with my mom's sorority sisters and close friends. They also talked about boys, caring for themselves, and makeup. Haelee's self-confidence began to sore as a direct result. I could finally take a break in rediscovering my peace of mind and finding myself again thanks to my mom's efforts. I started connecting with old friends, working out, reading, and enjoying life again. It appeared that God had smiled on us and brought us one step closer to Heaven. Haelee and I needed our own space however, so we moved out and into our own place in July 2017.

When the Going Gets Tough

I continued my therapeutic sessions throughout our transitions. Dr. Holtz was most impressed with how I was managing my condition and dealing with my traumas. She was happy to see that I was at peace. It did not last long unfortunately because Mrs. Richland and Ms. Rain approached me in September 2017, wanting Dr. Holtz to re-certify my need for reasonable accommodations. That seemed simple enough, but they asked for the same depth of information that they had previously requested and been provided. Not only that, but Mrs. Richland also went back on her word where she stated that I would not have to provide that depth of information again.

I followed up by contacting Dr. Holtz and making her aware of the situation at hand. She expressed frustration with Mrs. Richland's rigmarole. Dr. Holtz reminded me that she would not comply with their request unless I signed a HIPAA Release Form. She also reminded me that it was not in my best interest to sign it and that I should seek legal advice from an attorney. Notwithstanding she promised to take everything under consideration and follow up with me the following week regarding our next appointment and next steps. I did not hear back from her as promised so I reached out to her after two weeks went by to follow up. She unfortunately did not answer nor return my phone call. I reached out a few more times via email, telephone, and text message over the next few weeks but she never responded. I finally reached the conclusion that she had dropped me as a patient on October 9, 2017. That was a difficult day for me because I not only lost my medical provider but a friend as well due to Mrs. Richland and Ms. Rains shenanigans. While it was a difficult time, I knew that God did not bring me that far to let me down. As such,

I recalled the scripture, "To everything there is a season, and a time to every purpose under the heaven." (*The Holy Bible*, Ecclesiastes 3:1, NIV). What's more, I knew that I had more than enough to press on with the support of my mom and close friends. I mustered up the courage and informed Mrs. Richland and Ms. Rain that Dr. Holtz had dropped me as a patient and that it was their fault. I asked for some time to locate a new provider [one I could trust again] and they agreed to abate their RMI. They did not apologize for their fault in my losing my medical provider, however.

I found a new medical provider, Dr. Woods and I started meeting with her on January 25, 2018. She was incredibly down to earth, a great listener, and nonjudgmental. What's more, our connection was made easier because we share the same birthday of February 20. I was over the moon with joy when she shared that with me because I had only met one other person in life that shared my birthday. Ecclesiastes 3:1 came more into focus because of it all.

Moving along, Mrs. Richland reached out to me a few months later to inquire if I had found a new medical provider. I advised that I had but that she had not yet had enough time to establish an appropriate baseline regarding my diagnoses. Mrs. Richland said okay and reminded me that she and Ms. Rain would need that information. Notwithstanding she abated the RMI again. It remained in abatement until June 3, 2019, when Mrs. Richland requested an updated RMI. I cannot speak as to why she allowed it to remain in abatement for so long. I can only assume that it was due to underlying guilt where she and Ms. Rain caused me to lose my former medical provider through their shenanigans. At any rate, I was dumbfounded because she was doing exactly what she and Ms. Rain had done before in overreaching with respect to the information request and I was afraid. My fears were completely rational because Dr. Woods, echoed the same sentiments as Dr. Holtz previously. I worried myself to the point that I had yet another nervous breakdown. This one was much worse than the one that I had previously however because it required an inpatient hospital stay from June 21, 2019 to June 29, 2019. Haelee was at risk of going into temporary social services custody and our dog, Oreo was in danger of being sent to the kennel because I was not available to take care of or provide for them. My mom would not allow either of those things to happen hence she drove one hour to my house to pack them up and take them back to her house so that she could care for them despite her fear of driving on the highway. She was ever vigilant in taking care of them both while I was getting the therapeutic care that I needed.

The hospital was akin to being in prison because we were not allowed personal belongings unless they were thoroughly inspected by and approved by staff. They told us when to sleep, wake up, shower, etc. We were not even allowed in our rooms after 10:00 AM unless we had special permission from the doctor and the one bathroom in the area was locked with a key. To make matters worse, we were only allowed two visitors per week, one day per week, for 2 hours max. Above and beyond all of that, the staff members were extremely toxic and unprofessional. They would habitually antagonize patients so that they would get upset and act out in retaliation. Those that took the bait would have their stays extended. It was baffling to witness because it was not a long-term care hospital. Despite that fact, the hospital kept many of their patients for greater than 45-60 days. That made me wonder if I would ever get home to my daughter and our dog again.

While I did not have the privileges that I had at home, I was able to find a sense of peace because I found a Bible. I made sure to read it daily, especially Psalms 23 and Isaiah 40:31. Those two scriptures were/are ever-present reminders that we shall not fear. After all, God is and will be with us through everything. At any rate, the physician confirmed my already known and previously mentioned diagnoses while simultaneously diagnosing me with major depressive disorder (MDD). MDD is a persistent sense of despair and depression that lasts for at least two weeks. It can go on for as long as a few months to several years. That aside, he believed that I was stable enough to return home, so he coordinated with my mom to release me to her care on June 29, 2019. My mom, Haelee, and Oreo were sitting in the waiting room waiting for me upon my release. They met me with warm smiles and hugs as I burst into tears seeing them. My mom took me back to my house to clean myself up, grab some of my belongings, and took me back to her home. We stayed with her for a few weeks so that she could watch over us, particularly me.

Mrs. Richland submitted yet another RMI not long after I returned back to duty at work. I informed her that Dr. Woods and I were unwilling to provide the requested medical information. While that was the case, I advised her that I would be willing to undergo an independent psychological evaluation with a physician of her choosing since she appeared to be untrusting of my medical providers in the past. Mrs. Richland agreed to my request for an independent psychological evaluation, but she said that I would need to sign a HIPAA Release Form prior to her authorizing it. I was reluctant to sign it because I believed that doing so would allow her access to my protected medical file and data. Notwithstanding Mrs. Richland assured me that that would not happen, and that their physician only needed to talk with Dr. Woods to develop a baseline while conducting their independent assessment. My understanding was that an appointment would be setup for me to go see their selected physician after that so that they could perform the necessary evaluation. I relented and signed it so that we could move forward. I did not hear from Mrs. Richland again until November 2019. She told me that their contract with the National Institute of Health (NIH) had expired so she did not submit the original form. She further stated that the original form expired so she needed me to sign it again. I complied with her request by immediately signing it and sending it back to her on November 20, 2019. I did not hear a word back from Mrs. Richland or Ms. Rain until May 5, 2020. Ms. Rain sent me a letter on that day letting me know that my request for reasonable accommodations was denied and that I would need to start reporting to the office three days per week once the COVID-19 pandemic was over. Wait a minute, what???

CHAPTER 10: The Discrimination

You learned in the previous chapter that Ms. Rain made the decision to deny my request for continued reasonable accommodations. She provided this as defense for her decision, "**While the medical information confirmed your medical condition**, it did not sufficiently establish that you suffer from limitations that required a need to relocate to for medical care and treatment, and thus, full-time remote work is required to accommodate your symptoms by enabling you to perform the essential functions of your job. In fact, FOH discovered in its review that there were no medical limitations to you traveling and working in Washington, DC." A redacted copy of this letter is contained within Appendix 8.

Ms. Rain provided seven days to appeal her decision to my next line supervisor, Ms. Zenith if I was dissatisfied with her verdict. I responded by requesting a meeting with Ms. Rain that afternoon, and she agreed to meet with me. While my daughter and my experiences were none of her business, I intended on laying everything on the table concerning us. I had hoped that she would be empathetic towards our plight. I also wanted to find out how to appeal her decision if necessary. While she was gracious enough to meet with me, she was skeptical and apathetic with what I shared. She specifically said, "things were out of my hands once I pressed the send button. You will have to address matters with Ms. Zenith if you are dissatisfied." I, in turn, inquired what the appropriate protocol for doing so was. Ms. Rain told me to send her an email, let her know that I was disputing her decision, and request a meeting. I did precisely that, and Ms. Zenith agreed to meet with me on the following day.

Ms. Zenith and I met via Google Hangouts on the afternoon of May 6, 2020. She explained that we could not speak long because an all-hands meeting with the Agency Director was coming up soon. She also expressed a willingness to meet with me again on the following day should the need arise. I placed everything on the table concerning my disabilities and safety concerns for Haelee. It was not an easy conversation because I shared things with her that I have long kept hidden from family and friends. I questioned if things would work out in my favor, whether Ms. Zenith would believe that I was unfit for duty, or if she would attempt to place me in a compromising position as Ms. Anderson did previously [in Chapter 3]. I was completely overwhelmed with fear and emotion and resultantly had a panic attack. Ms. Zenith was the opposite of Ms. Rain in that she was both sympathetic and empathetic towards my plight. She gently apologized for leaving me to fend myself and promised that she would make time to speak with me again on May 7, 2020. She told me that she did not want to talk about the specifics of things and only wanted to hear about Haelee when we spoke again. She requested permission to access my human resources file before that next meeting, and I said okay through my panic.

Ms. Zenith and I met again on May 7, 2020, as promised. I started the meeting by attempting to tell her about Haelee; however, she cut me off much to my dismay. She retorted that she was only interested in what I was specifically requesting of her. She also tried to quiz me on my knowledge of the locality pay tables. To be specific, Ms. Zenith asked me if I was aware that I was overpaid while living in North Carolina. I told her that I was unaware while explaining that locality was associated with your reporting office, not where you lived. She grimaced, said that was incorrect, and inquired how I was unaware. I told her that I was unaware because I had updated my address in the payroll application and that the payroll office never said anything to me about changing my pay rate. She then asked me if I was familiar with the full-time telework policy. I told her that I was aware that it existed, but I was unfamiliar with its specifics, because I was not and never had been a full-time teleworker. I was a routine teleworker like every other employee in the Agency. I simply had an accommodation that afforded me to telework more than the typically allotted 2 - 3 days per week. Not only that, but neither of the Agency's reasonable accommodation policy, routine telework policy, nor my agreed accommodation contract made any mention of locality pay, proximity to headquarters, or anything of the sort. I apologized for my ignorance and offered to pay back the difference in salary if necessary [despite it being payrolls fault]. She retorted that she would take matters under careful consideration and that she had until May 21, 2020 to decide on my appeal. I thanked her for her time, and we concluded the call. I sent her an email on May 8, 2020, recapping exactly what was discussed in our meeting. A redacted copy of that email is located within Appendix 9.

Moving along, I filed a complaint with the Agency's EEO Office against Mrs. Richland and Ms.

Rain on May 7, 2020. The basis of my complaint was that they continuously requested wholly intrusive medical information, claimed that I did not have a disability that required accommodations, and that my reasonable accommodations effected my ability to meet the business needs of the division. The reference towards my ability to perform was most concerning to me as it was my first time hearing of those issues. What made it worse was that Ms. Rain and I met bi-weekly to discuss action plans, potential problems, and any other matter of the sort. Not only that but I received a rating of "**Exceeds Expectations**" on my mid-term performance review on May 18, 2020. To make matters worse, I also received a rating of "**Exceeds Expectations**" on my final performance evaluation on November 14, 2019. I received a performance award of $2,000 because of it and I was well on my way to receiving another one in 2020 had I continued to perform as I always had. With everything being said, it appeared that Ms. Rain was attempting to say that my disabilities and accommodations effected my ability to perform the essential duties of my job.

Moving forward, I received an email from Ms. Rain towards the conclusion of the business day on May 8, 2020 with a subject line of "decision documents." The first document was encrypted such that I could not open it. The second set of documents opened in a Google folder to which I had no access to. I resultantly submitted a request to access the folder. I received an email from the Human Resources Director, Ms. Marshall, on May 11, 2020, granting me access to the second set of documents. I was astonished by my findings. It was a 442-page document entitled "Evidence File." I naturally assumed that the evidence file was comprehensive given its length, but I was wrong as you will find out later. At any rate, Ms. Rain was proposing to terminate my [tenured] employment based on "Lack of Candor" and "Misuse of Government Equipment." She inferred that I relocated to North Carolina without requesting permission or notifying the Agency. On that note, she implied that I had been intentionally collecting Washington DC area pay while living in North Carolina for three years. I will not share my actual salary, but the difference in pay was approximately $11,000 per annum which came out to a $33,000 debt that I owed the Agency. The accusations were odd to me because I notified the Agency several times that I had relocated. I had literally updated my address in the employee directory and payroll system when I relocated to North Carolina in August 2016. I also notified the Agency's Office of Inspector General that I moved in April 2019 when I was a key witness in one of their investigations. I did so because the investigators wanted to meet with me in person. I told them that that was not possible because I worked from home and lived in another state. I subsequently asked them could we do the interview via Google Hangouts or telephone and they said "no, it has to be done in person." I retorted by asking the investigator how we would go about facilitating the interview and they said that they would drive down from Washington, DC to meet with me face-to-face. And finally, I told the Agency once again that I had moved when I submitted my eQIP and security clearance updates on March 2, 2020. The real issue was that the payroll office had failed to adjust my salary. Another problem was that I was unaware that I needed a salary adjustment in the first place. I will discuss that in more detail in the next chapter.

Moving forward, Ms. Rain accused me of misusing government equipment when I emailed County, State, and Federal Officials about my daughters' issues with the school and judicial system. The email records dated back to January 2016. She stated that while it was permissible to use my Agency email for personal use, I should have included a disclaimer indicating that I was not speaking on behalf of the government. I found that odd because while I was aware of that practice, I had never heard of it being necessary within the context I had used it in. This will also be discussed in greater detail in the next chapter.

Let the Games Begin

I amended my complaint to include retaliation on May 11, 2020. The Agency's EEO Office accepted my complaints and updates and assigned an EEO Specialist, Ms. Sylvia. She and I met on May 14, 2020, to discuss my concerns and desired remedies. My remedies were simply that, I wanted to be able to work remotely without fear of reprisal, repeated invasive RMI's, to be transferred to a position that no longer reported to Ms. Rain, and copies of the medical file that the Agency had obtained. Ms. Sylvia walked me through the next steps and my rights. They included the following

1. You have the right to remain anonymous during the informal process. Should you choose to remain anonymous, your anonymity is only protected during the informal stage of the complaint process. If you file a formal complaint, your anonymity is no longer protected.

2. You may be offered the option to participate in Alternative Dispute Resolution (ADR) instead of the traditional EEO counseling process at the time you determine to initiate informal counseling. Should you elect the ADR process you cannot later request traditional EEO counseling on the same matter.

3. While presenting or processing a discrimination complaint, you will be free from restraint, interference, coercion, harassment, discrimination, and reprisal.

4. You have the right to representation throughout the EEO complaint process, provided that your choice of a representative does not constitute a conflict of interest. If you designate an attorney as your representative, service of documents and decisions will be provided to your attorney and time of receipt shall be based upon the date your attorney receives such documents.

5. You have the right to file a formal complaint, a class complaint, and/or a civil action. Only the matters raised during informal counseling (or issues like or related to issues raised during

informal counseling) may be alleged in a subsequent complaint. The issues in the formal complaint, which were discussed with an EEO counselor, and/or the matter that gives rise to the complaint, must be sufficiently precise to describe generally the action(s) or practice(s) that form the basis of the complaint.

6. If you wish to file a formal complaint at the conclusion of counseling or ADR, you are required to file a formal complaint within 15 calendar days of receipt of the Notice of Right to File a Formal Complaint of Discrimination.

7. You have the right to request a hearing before an EEO Commission (EEOC) Administrative Judge (AJ). Once the investigation is completed, you have 30 days after you receive the investigative file to request a hearing before the AJ. If the investigation is not completed and you have not agreed to extend the period to complete the investigation, you may request a hearing at any time after 180 days has elapsed from the filing of the complaint.

8. You have the right to file a civil action in a U.S. District Court 180 calendar days after filing a formal complaint or 180 calendar days after filing an appeal with the EEOC.

9. If you are alleging sex-based wage discrimination under the Equal Pay Act (EPA), you have the right to go directly to a U.S. District Court even though such claims may be filed and processed under Title VII of the Civil

Rights Act of 1964, as amended. A civil action must be filed within 2 years of the date of the occurrence, or within 3 years of the date of an alleged willful violation.

10. You have the right to file a civil action in a U.S. District Court under the Age Discrimination in Employment Act (ADEA) after giving the EEOC no less than 30 days' notice of intent to file such an action. The notice must be filed in writing with the EEOC within 180 days of the occurrence of the alleged unlawful practice. The notice must be submitted to the EEOC, Office of Federal Operations, ATTN: Hearing Programs Division; P.O. Box 77960; Washington, DC 20013.

11. You have the right to request compensatory damages at any stage of the discrimination complaint process, including at the informal stage. Compensatory damages constitute pecuniary (out-of-pocket) and nonpecuniary (as mental or emotional harm) losses which are the direct result of a discriminatory act.

12. You are entitled to request a reasonable amount of official time to prepare or otherwise work on presentation of your formal complaint. Requests for such leave should be made in advance to your supervisor, in the same manner that requests for annual and sick leave are accomplished. What is a "reasonable amount of time" is determined on a case-by-case basis, and

normally is based upon the length of time required to address your complaint.

Ms. Sylvia explained the differences between Traditional EEO Counseling vs. ADR. Traditional EEO Counseling is a complex process that requires an official investigation. Agencies are allotted 180 days from the date of complaint filing to complete their respective investigations. The investigators go back and forth between the respective parties to gather relevant facts for associated complaints. Agencies issue notices following the conclusion of these investigations. That notice provides complainants an opportunity to either request a hearing with an EEOC AJ or for the Agency to decide whether discrimination occurred. Agencies are more likely to say that discrimination did not happen unless it is extreme and grossly negligent because the investigators work for them. With that in mind, you should always request a hearing. At issue, however, is that the price of hearings typically exceeds $10,000.

ADR is facilitated mediation. It allows competing parties to reach agreements that are mutually beneficial to both sides. It is accomplished through the aid of a neutral arbitrator as opposed to a EEOC AJ. ADR helps reduce costs because it eliminates litigation, hearings, and investigations It also minimizes the usage of Official Agency time. It is pretty much a win-win proposition in that respect. I made the decision to select ADR because I believed it most appropriate and beneficial for both sides.

Moving forward, Ms. Zenith sent me an email on May 22, 2020, stating that she had chosen to uphold Ms. Rain's [ridiculous] decision to revoke my accommodations. I did not stress over it because that simply added more credence to my complaint. I thanked her for her time and updated my complaint accordingly. I reached out to my AFGE Union Representative, Ms. Hall and asked her to represent me in mediation. She informed me that she would not be able to do so because the Trump Administration had performed a litany of moves to weaken the Union and had done so to the detriment of employees. Some of those items included allowing discipline without bargaining, limiting employee rights to organize and engage in collective bargaining, limiting employee rights to communicate about workplace issues, reducing official union time, and charging AFGE and other Unions rent for office space usage. While that was most concerning, I did not stress over it because you can have anyone represent you. I subsequently reached out to a friend, Ms. Butler and asked if she would represent me. She said "yes, of course." Ms. Butler is not an attorney, but she boasts a Doctorate of Speech Pathology and Master of Education, is a Dean at an institution of higher learning, knows me very well, and would look out for my best interests.

Moving forward, Ms. Williams, Sr. EEO Specialist, reached out to me on June 12, 2020, to advise that the Agency had agreed to ADR, and that they had appointed Ms. Turnbill as the mediator. She also stated that mediation had to be completed by August 5, 2020, as it would have in effect been 90 days after I had filed my initial complaint. Ms. Turnbill followed up on June 15, 2020, informing us that she was available on either July 14, 2020, or July 16, 2020, at 9:30 AM to facilitate our mediation session(s). The assigned management officials, Ms. Nibble, Ms. Butler, and I, all responded that we were available on July 14, 2020. Ms. Turnbill thanked us for responding and scheduled the session accordingly. Ms. Butler and I commenced preparing for my defense and settlement negotiations immediately thereafter. The Agency's attorney, Ms. Lawrence, Esq responded on July 22, 2020 however in saying that she had a schedule conflict so she would be unable to attend. She inquired about any other availability, and I responded by informing her that my representative, was unavailable for representation after July 14, 2020. Ms. Lawrence was understanding and made a counteroffer on June 25, 2020, to meet on July 10, 2020, at 1:00 PM and we agreed to that date. Ms. Turnbill sent out an updated meeting invite for all of us to accept and we did for the most part. Ms. Nibble responded later that afternoon by saying that she would be on vacation from July 6, 2020 – July 10, 2020 hence she would be unable to attend. She then inquired if there were any other available dates. Ms. Turnbill retorted that she could facilitate on either July 16, 2020, or July 27, 2020. Both dates were unacceptable because Ms. Butler would not be available as previously prefaced. On that premise, I asked that we stick to the previously agreed-upon date of July 14, 2020. Ms. Lawrence reiterated that she would be unable to attend due to a scheduling conflict. Ms. Turnbill resultantly inquired if either August 3, 2020, or August 4, 2020, would suffice. I advised her that it would not, and that meeting on those dates would not allow sufficient time for us to reach a mutually beneficial agreement given the time constraints of ADR. Frustrated by all the back and forth, I decided to consult with and hire an attorney, Alan Lescht and Associates, PC. I paid the requisite retainer and let the Agency know that Ms. Slater, Esq would be representing me as opposed to Ms. Butler going forward. Ms. Lawrence's response was, "seeing as scheduling will be a challenge, let's proceed with the original date, and I will have a different Agency counsel step in if necessary."

Ms. Slater and I filed a petition with the Merit Systems Protection Board (MSPB) on July 8, 2020 as a leverage technique. The MSPB is, "an independent, quasi-judicial agency in the Executive Branch that serves as the guardian of Federal merit systems." (*U.S. Merit Systems Protection Board - About*). They adjudicate employee appeals that fall within their jurisdiction; hence they serve as a federal court of sorts. As stated previously, it is costly to file a federal lawsuit. Notwithstanding, employees hold the advantage when cases are presented before the MSPB because the burden of proof resides with the Agency. Not only that, but lawsuits require an abundance of resource time from Agency personnel. That aside, Ms. Slater and I advised Ms. Lawrence that we would drop the petition in exchange for the remedies that I had previously requested. Ms. Slater also instructed me to draft a victim impact statement. She said that she would start the mediation with an overview of my case.

I would then present my victim impact statement to be followed by settlement negotiations.

Ms. Thornbill, Ms. Lawrence, Ms. Nibble, Ms. Slater, and I met on July 14, 2020 at 9:30 AM. I recited my impact statement following the introductions and case overview. In short, I stated how working for Ms. Rain was triggering in that it was causing me to suffer from insomnia and depression. I further shared how she had repeatedly discriminated against and proposed terminating me following my filing of the EEO Complaint. A redacted version of that statement is contained within Appendix 10. Ms. Thornbill suggested that we proceed with negotiations after that. Ms. Slater and I followed by presenting a series of offers. Ms. Lawrence and Nibble rejected each one of them, however. They chose to finger point and argue with Ms. Slater and myself instead of negotiating or presenting counter offers. We realized in short order that the Agency had no intent to operate in good faith, particularly when they expressed an unwillingness to provide the medical file that they had obtained. Given that sentiment, we chose to conclude the session early and proceeded with our appeal to the MSPB. I will discuss this in more detail in the next chapter.

CHAPTER 11: A Dreary Court Battle

As mentioned previously, Ms. Rain had proposed my termination without my knowledge. I found out when I received a ticket from the IT Service Desk on June 5, 2020. I was sure that it was an error, so I reached out to Ms. Zenith for clarity via email. She unfortunately did not reply to my original email. She sent me a letter under a different heading explaining that I was being terminated under the guise of "Lack of Candor" and "Misuse of Government Equipment." She provided in that letter that Ms. Rain had given me fifteen days from May 8, 2020 to respond in opposition to her accusations and that I had neglected to do so. She proffered that my failure to oppose the accusations was an admission of guilt and acceptance of Ms. Rain's proposed termination order. I informed Ms. Zenith that I did not receive the letter that she was referring to hence I was unable to respond as appropriate. She did not respond, however. It did not matter though because the damage had already been done. I followed up by notifying Ms. Sylvia that I had been terminated and that I would need to update my EEO Complaint to further reflect [illegal] retaliation. Ms. Sylvia agreed and offered to conclude ADR and let me go ahead and file an official EEO Complaint wherein the Agency would launch an official investigation. Ms. Slater suggested that we drop the EEO Case; however, in favor of pursuing legal remedies through the MSPB. The logic in doing so was that we could take matters directly to them without first having completed an investigation. Given that sentiment it would be a much quicker process because the MSPB resolves all matters within 120 days. EEO Cases on the other hand can take up to a year if not more given that 180 days are allotted towards investigations. Ms. Slater followed this up by filing an appeal with the MSPB on July 2, 2020. Our arguments were as follows:

1. The Agency failed to meet its evidentiary burden.

2. Removal did not promote the efficiency of the federal service.

3. Removal was unreasonable pursuant to the Douglas factors.

4. The Agency violated Appellant's due process rights when it failed to provide him with Notice of his Proposed removal.

5. The Agency's actions constituted unlawful retaliation.

The MSPB filed an acknowledgement order and assigned Judge Mehring as the AJ on July 8, 2020. An acknowledgement order confirms receipt of appeals. It also establishes the processes and procedures for hearings. Judge Mehring sent an electronic copy of the appeal to the agency and directed them to submit their evidence file along with their justification for their actions. The Agency's attorney, Mr. Pop, Esq acknowledged the Agency's mistake with respect to violating my due process rights on July 13, 2020. He made amends by having Ms. Zenith retract her termination order effective June 5, 2020. He explained that I would receive back pay, benefits, and associated emoluments. Ms. Slater and I subsequently dropped the appeal on July 10, 2020. While that was good news, the battle was far from over as you will learn in the pages to follow. A redacted version of that document is contained within Appendix 11.

Ms. Rain sent out a new proposal for termination on July 23, 2020. She did so under a new guise of "Failure to Work from an Approved Duty Station" in addition to lack of candor and misuse of government equipment. She afforded us 22 calendar days from the date of transmission to respond to her proposal. That meant that we had to provide a defense by August 14, 2020 at the latest. I was concerned that she had added another charge. It pretty much appeared that the Agency was throwing everything against the wall to see what would stick. Ms. Slater said that while that appeared to be true, they were legally able to do so because the original proposal to terminate was no longer relevant. She nor I belabored those points however, we simply started working on my defense.

Ms. Slater sent our written defense via email to Mr. Pop and Ms. Zenith on August 14, 2020. She went into detail within on how the Agency could not meet its evidentiary burden, terminating me would not promote the efficiency of federal service, the penalty of removal was unreasonable for a first-time offense, the Agency's actions constituted unlawful discrimination and retaliation, and highlighting my outstanding performance record throughout the entirety of my career. Based on those factors, she stated that the proposal had to be rescinded with restoration of my reasonable accommodations particularly given that we were in the middle of a global pandemic. Ms. Zenith confirmed receipt of our defense and stated that she would thoroughly review it. It was an overall strong case hence I assumed that everything was over and that we would all be moving forward soon.

The Long Painful Journey

I was visiting with Ms. Butler and her family on August 25, 2020. I saw a vehicle approaching in my rear-view mirror as I turned off the side street that she lives on as I was leaving to return home. I realized that the other driver was going too fast and that they were going to rear end me if I did not get out of the way. I switched lanes to get out of their way only to find out that they had the same thought process. They literally changed lanes right behind me only this time they were ever closer and coming fast. I attempted to switch lanes yet again when I heard a loud blast. Things went black immediately thereafter. A bright, white light appeared in time and it awakened me. I could see my car on the median strip, dashing headfirst into oncoming traffic. I slammed on my brakes, but my car continued to drift. It happened upon me to pull my parking brake up and my car finally came to a stop. I was less than a foot away from oncoming traffic.

My neck, back, and shoulder began to hurt not long after I came to a stop. Nonetheless, I gave up a quick shout of praise as I knew that it was nobody but God, who saved me from sure death or severe injury. Things went black again after that. I was awakened again by a witness who knocked on my window. He let me know that he had called 911 and that the police were on the way. He then inquired if I needed medical assistance. I thanked him for calling the police, and I told him that I would call the paramedics myself.

I called Ms. Butler and advised her that I had been in an accident. I asked her if she could come and pick me up. She retorted that she would, and she requested my whereabouts. I responded that I was unsure but that I was somewhere near her house. Ms. Butler inquired how could I not know where I was. I could only respond that I did not know while reiterating that I was not far away from her house. Ms. Butler said that she and her dad, were on their way and that they would find me one way or the other. I finally called 911 after we hung up and requested medical assistance. I was in severe pain and extremely tired, so I kept falling asleep. The dispatcher implored me to stay awake while simultaneously requesting my location. I told the dispatcher that I was unsure of my whereabouts and that I simply needed help. They told me to just stay awake and that they would find me via location services on my phone. Three Caucasian paramedics approached my car a short time thereafter. They began to question me, take my vitals, and tend to my injuries. While they were friendly, I was deftly afraid of them because racial tensions in the country were extremely high and I was defenseless given my injuries. I was on the verge of having yet another panic attack when Mr. Butler arrived. He implored me to allow the paramedics to do their job and advised that he was keeping a close eye on them. I said okay and my anxiety began to subside because I felt safe with him there. They placed a brace around my neck, took an accident report, and offered to take me to the emergency room.

I refused to comply however because it was getting late, and Haelee was at home by herself. The paramedics stated that I was putting myself at risk for paralysis given the scope of my injuries, so they implored me to reconsider. I refused because I could not take care of myself without first ensuring that my daughter was safe. I asked Ms. Butler if she could take me home and she said that she would. I told the paramedics that I would go to the emergency room in the morning if my condition did not improve. The paramedics said that they would be legally liable for leaving me to my vices given my condition. They were not willing to take that chance hence they asked me to sign a waiver of responsibility after realizing that I had no intentions of allowing them to transport me. I signed the waiver as requested and they helped me out of my vehicle and into the rear of Ms. Butler's car.

My pain became more intense as Ms. Butler pulled off. She emphatically said that I could not afford to wait until the next morning to go to the emergency room and that she was taking me immediately whether I liked it or not. I reiterated that I did not want to leave Haelee by herself all night. Ms. Butler told me not to worry about it because she would go to my house and stay with her after she dropped me off at the emergency room. She shared that I could simply call her when I was ready and that she and Haelee would come and pick me up. I thanked her and I went to sleep as she slowly drove me to emergency room. We finally arrived and she let me out the car. She reminded me to preserve my cell phone battery so that I could call her when I was ready. I sat in the hospital waiting room for what seemed like an eternity. Here I was not only injured but with my career up in the air as well. I asked myself, "can life get any worse than this" as I reflected on my ordeal.

Three hours went by before the nurse called me back for a consultation and MRI. The MRI was complete in 5 minutes, and the results came an hour after that. The results were that I had a collapsed disk in my neck, whiplash, and a pinched nerve in my shoulder. The physician gave me a prescription and ordered me to follow up with their neurosurgeon within the next three days. I reached out to the neurosurgeon's office on August 28, 2020. They made an appointment for me to come in on September 2, 2020. My right shoulder was most troubling because my pain was most intense there. It was a literal struggle to shower, brush my teeth, feed myself, etc. because I am right-handed. I felt hopeless as I pondered if I would ever be whole again. At any rate, the day of my appointment finally arrived, and the neurosurgeon said that surgery would not be required right away. He referred me to physical therapy and pain management instead. He communicated that he preferred to take the least invasive path in helping people return to health. While that was good news, I was not out of the woods yet because he said that surgery would be required if the alternatives did not work. I should have been happy at receiving the news, but I was just too deep in a pool of depression because of everything. My cousin, Mr. Ruxsakriskul and several of my friends, Mr. Ford, Ms. Lewis, Mr. Johnson, Ms. Pierre, Ms. Curry, and Ms. Ahmad were extremely worried about me. They resultantly got together and took it upon themselves to try and lift me out of my funk. They sent gifts, food, and money to ensure that Haelee and I were eating. Mr. Ford even drove down from Maryland, to check on me in person, gave me a get-well-soon gift, and taught Haelee how to care for me if I refused to take care of myself.

Moving forward, I took Haelee to the hair salon and shared with her that we could have dinner from a restaurant of her choice on September 11, 2020. I decided to check my email while I waited in the parking lot. I saw that I had an unread email from Mr. Pop on behalf of Ms. Zenith. It stated within that she was upholding the termination decision, that my final day of employment would be September 18, 2020, and that I had 30 days to appeal the decision to the MSPB. I was disheartened as I knew it would cost thousands of dollars to go that route. Not only that, but it was clear that she did not truly consider any of our defenses with respect to her responses. She simply held to the premise that I sent the emails without considering the critical context of that I did so to protect Haelee's life. She also held to the premise that I had violated the full-time telework policy when I was never a full-time teleworker.

I applied for unemployment in hopes that it would help offset the loss of income while we worked through the process of the appeal and my looking for another job. I also applied for disability if unemployment did not work out. I was saddened to find out that I was ultimately denied for both. What was odd was that I was afforded an opportunity to appeal the latter but not the former. While I was well within my rights to appeal my claim for disability, I declined to do so because I did not want to go through that headache. Effective appeals require the aid of an attorney and I simply could not afford one given that I was already paying several thousand dollars towards Alan Lescht and Associates for Ms. Slater's representation. I shook my head and pondered what else could go wrong. The good news was that I had always been proactive as opposed to reactive hence I always planned for a rainy day. I simply took money out of savings so that Haelee and I could maintain a decent standard of living. But not only that, I took out enough so that I could continue to pay for my legal defense. The larger issue was my loss of health insurance. I rectified that however in filing for and being approved for Medicaid. Our case worker was kind enough to approve us for the Supplemental Nutrition Assistance Program (SNAP) as well after finding out what had happened to us. It was difficult for me to accept these things due to pride. I put it aside and accepted it however because it was a time for humility and gratitude.

Over and beyond everything, I pondered if my ex-wife would use my fragile circumstances to request a custody modification in trying to take Haelee away from me. She instead assured me that she had faith in me and that she had no doubt that things would work out in my favor. She prefaced that Haelee was in good hands with me and that she would not try and take her away from me. While I was still unemployed and injured, I had faced and overcome my greatest fear, losing my daughter.

Moving along, everything began to take a toll on me, so I sunk further into depression. Haelee had been asking me for several weeks when I was going back to work. I responded by giving her a different excuse each time. She retorted that she did not see why it was so hard for me to go back to work despite my injuries since I worked from home. I finally ran out of excuses over time and I decided that I needed to simply be honest with her. I did not know how to deliver the news however, but I needed to figure it out. I wondered if she would think any less of me in finding out that I had lost my job. I worried myself to the point of anxiety as I attempted to come up with various ways of delivering the news. I finally decided to just tell her over dinner on September 26, 2020. I shared with her that she might have noticed that I had been depressed over the past several weeks and that my depression was not totally linked towards my injuries. I did not go into any specific details, but I shared with her that I had lost my job. I also shared with her that I understood that it was close to her birthday and that she had big plans for it but that I could not afford anything big given my financial situation. I burst into tears following my reveal as I felt like a complete failure. Haelee amazed me because she took the news with grace and responded with a message that showed that she was wise beyond her years. She said, "It's okay Dad. I believe in you. We're going to be okay. We've been through so much worse before. You should focus on what you have like your eyesight, your ability to walk, the roof over our head, the people that love you, and just being alive instead of what you have lost. God didn't bring us this far to see you fall. You must believe that He's going to bring us through it. And besides, I have never seen you lose a case. You always win in court." I cried in her arms in amazement because Haelee became the parent for that moment. Her message gave me the encouragement to pull myself up and fight on.

Selah

I would like you to take a moment to reflect. 2020 was rough for everyone but if you are alive, then you survived it. You must trust and believe that things will be okay and that you are going to make it. Please do not allow yourself to become entrapped within the spirit of despair. Please focus on Haelee's wise words of focusing on what you do have like your eyesight, your ability to walk, the roof over your head, the people who love you, and being alive rather than focusing on what you lost. God did not bring you this far to see you fall. You must believe that He's going to bring you through all things.

Burn Baby, Burn

Ms. Slater filed a new appeal with respect to my termination on October 2, 2020. She argued:

1. The Agency failed to meet its evidentiary burden.

2. Removal did not promote the efficiency of the federal service.

3. Removal was unreasonable pursuant the Douglas factors.

4. The Agency's actions constituted unlawful discrimination based on disability.

5. The Agency's actions constituted unlawful retaliation.

The MSPB acknowledged our appeal and assigned a new AJ, Judge Zamora on October 13, 2020. As mentioned previously, an acknowledgement order forwards a copy of an appeal to an agency while simultaneously ordering them to submit a copy of their evidence file. Mr. Pop complied as directed by transmitting it on November 2, 2020. Judge Zamora followed that up by setting the order for the appeal on November 3, 2020. The order for the appeal was as follows:

1. Status Conference

2. Prehearing Submission

3. Prehearing Conference

4. Hearing

The AJ facilitates status conferences. They expect each party to be intimately familiar with the facts and issues surrounding the appeal to include any potential motions, settlement offers, orders to compel, and status of discovery. Our status conference was originally scheduled for November 10, 2020; however,

Mr. Pop waited until the afternoon of November 6, 2020 to claim that he would be unable to attend due to a previously scheduled medical procedure. He subsequently requested that it be rescheduled. Judge Zamora honored his request by rescheduling the conference for November 12, 2020. She led Ms. Slater, Mr. Pop, and I in a discussion regarding the issues under appeal. She followed up by inquiring about our attempts at settlement. Mr. Pop inferred that we had not engaged in any type of settlement discussions because he had not received an offer from either Ms. Slater or I. Ms. Slater countered that we sent a settlement offer on October 25, 2020 yet received no response to it. Mr. Pop retorted that he did not see it to which Ms. Slater responded that she would forward it over again at the conclusion of the status conference.

Discovery is a process that is used to uncover helpful facts and documents with respect to a case. Motions for discovery had to be served no later than November 12, 2020. Responses to it were due no later than December 2, 2020. Judge Zamora resultantly inquired how discovery was going. Ms. Slater retorted that we were putting the finishing touches on the Agency's discovery request and that we would be responding to it by the due date. Mr. Pop responded that he was working on it and that he would be responding to our discovery request soon.

Moving along, the Civil Service Reform Act of 1978, Pub. L. No. 95-454, 92 Stat. 1111 protects federal employees and applicants from retaliation when they exercise rights such as filing an EEO Complaint, Grievance, etc. With that in mind, Judge Zamora stated that her understanding was that we were claiming reprisal and disability discrimination within the scope of our appeal. Ms. Slater confirmed that she was correct. Judge Zamora retorted that we would need to develop an affirmative defense argument that supported our claims and that it would be due by December 10, 2020. An affirmative defense argument must show that an employee, "engaged in a statutorily-protected activity; he or she was subsequently treated adversely by the agency; the deciding official (the person authorized to make the final decision on a disciplinary action) had actual or constructive knowledge that the employee engaged in the protected activity; and a causal connection exists between the protected activity and the personnel action." (*U.S. Merit Systems Protection Board - Prohibited Personnel Practices*).

Ms. Slater started working on the affirmative defense argument on December 2, 2020. She was unable to complete it as scheduled however because Mr. Pop failed to respond to our request for discovery by the assigned due date. He claimed time and again after the due date that he would be delivering it soon, yet he failed to do so or provide a specific date as to when he would. Ms. Slater informed him that she would be filing a request for an extension and a motion to compel after receiving the run around with no guarantees on the expected delivery date. A motion to compel is where either the Appellant or the Agency requests the judge to enforce a request for discovery through the issuance of a subpoena. Mr. Pop finally promised that he would have a response over to us no later than December 9, 2020. Ms. Slater said okay and refrained from filing the motion to compel. She did file a request for extension however because she did not have enough time to draft the affirmative defense argument as appropriate. The arguments were as follows:

1. On November 12, 2020, Appellant and the Agency served discovery requests.

2. Appellant included specific discovery requests related to Appellant's disability discrimination affirmative defense, the subject of the Affirmative Defense statement.

3. On December 2, 2020, Appellant served discovery responses.

4. On December 3, 2020, undersigned counsel contacted Agency counsel about the Agency's discovery responses, as they had not been produced.

5. On December 3, 2020, Agency counsel responded stating that the Agency did "intend to respond soon."

6. On December 4, 2020, Appellant contacted Agency counsel asking when the Agency intended to provide discovery responses. It was further noted that, if the Agency's responses were not provided by December 7, 2020, undersigned counsel would seek an extension for the Affirmative Defense statement – due on December 10, 2020.

7. The Agency's discovery responses are essential for Appellant to be able to file a comprehensive Affirmative Defense statement.

8. On December 7, 2020, undersigned counsel asked Agency counsel whether the Agency would consent to the instant motion.

9. On December 8, 2020, Agency counsel consented to the instant motion, and notified undersigned counsel that the Agency intends to provide discovery responses by December 9, 2020.

10. Pursuant to the November 12, 2020 Affirmative Defense Order, the Appellant's current deadline to file an Affirmative Defense statement is December 10, 2020.

Judge Zamora found our argument to be acceptable within the auspices of good cause. Good cause is, "a legally sufficient reason for a ruling or other action by a judge." (*Hill and Hill The people's law dictionary: taking the mystery out of legal language*). She resultantly granted our request for an extension until December 18, 2020. She further proffered that she would be willing to approve a motion to compel if the Agency did not respond by their promised delivery date of December 9, 2020. She stated that the motion would need to be entered by either Ms. Slater or myself by December 12, 2020 if needed. Mr. Pop held true to his word in responding on December 9, 2020 as promised hence there was no need to enter the motion. Ms.

Slater followed up by finalizing and submitting the affirmative defense argument on December 18, 2020 as scheduled. Our defense contained a statement of facts in addition to supporting arguments. Several of those facts are provided below.

1. In July 2015, Appellant had a panic attack at the worksite, and requested to telework part-time as a Reasonable Accommodation

2. In August 2015, Appellant began teleworking part time.

3. On February 4, 2016, Appellant request full-time telework as a RA due to Appellant's specific diagnosis, and the stressors of his commute into the Washington, D.C. office.

4. On June 14, 2016, Appellant's request for full-time telework was granted.

5. On September 17, 2019, the Office of Inspector General ("OIG") sent Rain a memorandum stating that Appellant "may have misused his position and government email address;" "misused the workforce mobility and telework policies, and as a result received Washington, D.C., locality pay while living and working in North Carolina;" and "failed to provide updated medical documentation necessary to perform an annual review of his reasonable accommodation

6. In or around September 2017, the Agency requested additional medical documentation about Appellant's RA

7. The appellant requested those medical documents from his medical provider in or around October 2017. His medical provider chose not to comply and dropped Appellant as a client instead. This was emotionally damaging to the Appellant as he had been a client since 2014.

8. In or around January 2018, Appellant relayed to the Agency that his medical provider, was unwilling to provide the requested medical information because the previously provided information was sufficient, and the request was otherwise too expansive.

9. Appellant further explained that his medical provider would refer Appellant to a new practitioner if the Agency insisted on the additional documentation that she was unwilling to provide.

10. Appellant also states that Mrs. Richland verbally told him in or around April 2016 that he would not need to provide in depth medical information again because she would place the already existing in depth information in his personnel file.

11. In or around April 2019, the Office of Inspector General ("OIG") interviewed

Appellant as a witness in an investigation for which Appellant was not the subject. Appellant voluntarily disclosed to the OIG investigator that he lived in North Carolina.

12. On June 6, 2019, Appellant asked his supervisor at the time – if he could apply for full-time telework outside of the Reasonable Accommodation process. She told him that he could not because he has a disability and an accommodation agreement.

13. On July 8, 2019, Appellant authorized the disclosure of medical information to the Federal Occupational Health Service (FOH), Department of Health and Human Services (HHS), to confirm his diagnoses for his RA. Mrs. Richland reached out to the Appellant sometime in November 2019 and let him know that the Agency's contract with FOH had expired so she never submitted the authorization for disclosure of medical information. She asked the Appellant to sign the form and resubmit them to her on November 19, 2019 and again on November 20, 2019 and he complied.

14. On May 5, 2020, Ms. Rain revoked Appellant's full-time telework accommodation, stating that a FOH review of Appellant's medical records found that there were **"no medical limitations" to Appellant travelling to Washington, D.C. for work, even though**

his medical provider stated as a part of that same review that she was "not aware of any problems of [Appellant] performing [his] job duties as long as [he] work[s] from home."

15. On May 5, 2020, Appellant told Ms. Rain that he would be filing an appeal and grievance against Mrs. Richland and herself.

16. On May 6, 2020, Appellant asked Zenith to reconsider.

17. On May 7, 2020 Appellant filed an EEOC complaint alleging discrimination based on Rain's revocation of Appellant's RA.

18. On May 8, 2020, Appellant received an email from Ms. Rain entitled "Decision Documents." The email included encrypted attachments. When Appellant requested unencrypted versions of the documents so that he could access them, he was only sent the Evidence File by Ms. Marshall on May 11, 2020.

19. On May 11, 2020, Appellant amended his EEO Complaint to include retaliation for protected activity.

20. On May 21, 2020, Ms. Zenith affirmed the denial of Appellant's RA.

21. On June 5, 2020, Appellant received a Decision from Ms. Zenith stating that she had affirmed

Ms. Rain's Proposal to Remove Appellant. Appellant had not, however, received that Proposal, and therefore had not responded to it.

22. On July 9, 2020, the Initial Removal Decision was rescinded, because Appellant had not received proper notice of the proposal.

23. On September 11, 2020, Ms. Zenith issued a Decision affirming the Proposed Removal.

We argued that a preponderance of evidence affirmed that I was a qualified individual with a disability, that the Agency subjected me to adverse treatment, and that the adverse treatment gave rise to an inference of discrimination. Given those sentiments we specifically argued that we had established a prima facie case for discrimination. Prima facie is defined as, "a party produces evidence that unless rebutted is sufficient to prove a particular proposition or fact." (*U.S. Merit Systems Protection Board - Prohibited Personnel Practices*). We also argued that I had established a prima facie case for retaliation because I had engaged in a protected activity, the Agency knew about the protected activity, the Agency subjected me to adverse treatment, and that there was a causal connection between the protected activity and the adverse treatment.

Moving forward, the Agency informed us that they had no intentions on settling the appeal on December 14, 2020. As such we pressed forward with our request for a hearing. Judge Zamora opined that the prehearing submission needed to be completed by December 30, 2020. This consisted of a statement of facts, a list of witnesses, expected witness testimony, and a copy of indexed exhibits. This was to be followed by a prehearing conference on January 5, 2021. A prehearing conference outlines the scope of a hearing to include the exchanging of exhibits, conduct and disposition, and obtaining the respective arguments by opposing parties. Discovery was ordered to effectively terminate on that date. Judge Zamora was then to lead us in a review and discussion of the provided materials. She also expected us to come prepared to discuss our efforts to settle matters [once again], to define the issues, and to reach stipulations of uncontested facts.

Solid as a Rock

The hearing was scheduled for January 8, 2021. Ms. Slater had been my representative counsel throughout the entire ordeal, but she was an associate attorney. While she worked on cases that involved employment discrimination, she lacked trial experience in that regard. She subsequently exited the case and turned it over to Ms. McDonough on December 21, 2020. Ms. McDonough had trial experience in representing government clients in cases before the MSPB, EEOC, and State Courts to include discrimination, reprisal, due process, and sexual harassment. What's more, Ms. McDonough is/was, "recognized by Super Lawyers as a top-rated employment litigation attorney in Washington DC." (*Sara McDonough*). Ms. McDonough and I decided to request a decision on the written record as opposed to

106

having an official hearing, however. A decision on the written record is akin to an appellant brief in that it contains the issues of dispute, statements of fact, and arguments in support of the appellant's position. It makes the argument as to why the appellant should win the case. We reached this decision because it was the most cost-effective solution. What's more, we believed that the case was strong enough to be decided on the merits of written facts alone. Another factor that we considered was that hearings that include witness testimony can often cost an additional $10,000. Ms. McDonough resultantly informed Judge Zamora of our decision and requested a close of record order on December 30, 2020. A close of record order effectively concludes discovery in legal proceedings.

Mr. Pop submitted his pre-hearing report on December 30, 2020. The report contained a statement of facts, defenses, and exhibits. He continued to contend that I had violated stipulations of the full-time telework policy within the context of the report. It was perplexing and ironic because I never was a full-time teleworker as previously prefaced. The irony of it all was that the Agency's own evidence file supported my being a routine teleworker. The Agency also finally turned over copies of the medical file that we had repeatedly requested since May 6, 2020.

Judge Zamora honored our request for a close of record order on December 31, 2020. She provided that all previously provided evidence was then a part of the record and ordered that it not be resubmitted. She also provided that both parties could submit additional evidence that they wanted considered so long is it contained a certificate of service that a copy was provided to the opposing party up until January 8, 2021. She followed this all up by cancelling the previously scheduled prehearing conference and hearing. She then set a due date for the appellant brief of January 13, 2021.

Ms. McDonough began work on my appellate brief on January 4, 2021. She submitted it to Judge Zamora on January 13, 2021 along with a sworn affidavit from me. She started it off by stating that I suffered from anxiety, panic disorder, and agoraphobia. She then borrowed from the affirmative action defense in highlighting the most critical points of note from it. She argued that I had successfully performed and, in most cases, exceeded my duties throughout my career with the federal government despite my disabilities. She further highlighted how a classmate and community member had repeatedly physically assaulted, sexually assaulted, and spread sexually based rumors about my daughter. She expounded upon that to include the fact that Haelee developed school phobia and agoraphobia due to broken trust in the school system and its authorities due to their failures to protect her. Worst of all, she noted how Haelee became depressed and even contemplated suicide. With that said, she argued that I did what any good parent would do in getting their child help and that I did that by relocating us both.

Ms. McDonough provided the applicable legal standards from there. The legal standards were

> The Agency bears the burden of proving that Appellant was removed "only for such cause as

will promote the efficiency of the service." 5 U.S.C. § 7513(a). In order to satisfy its burden of proof, the Agency must prove three independent elements by a preponderance of the evidence. Id. at §7513(a) and § 7701(c)(1)(B). Preponderant evidence is the degree of relevant evidence that a reasonable person, considering the record as a whole, would accept as sufficient to find that a contested fact is more likely to be true than untrue. See 5 C.F.R. § 1201.56(c)(2).

First, the Agency must prove that Appellant engaged in misconduct as specifically alleged in the Proposed Removal. See Fitzgerald v. Dep't of the Army, 61 MSPR 426, 428 (1994). Second, the Agency must "show the connection or 'nexus' between the charges and the impact on the efficiency of the Agency." See 5 U.S.C. § 7513(b); 5 C.F.R. § 752.301; see also Kruger v. Dep't of Justice, 32 MSPR 71, 74, (1987). Third, the Agency must prove that the penalty of removal is reasonable under the circumstances of the case. See 5 U.S.C. § 7513(b); 5 C.F.R. § 752.301.

Ms. McDonough argued that the agency failed to meet their evidentiary burden that I engaged in misconduct. Her statement in that regard was based upon the fact that the Agency must prove that I engaged in misconduct as stated within Fitzgerald v Dep't of the Army. 61 MSPR 426 (1994). With that in mind, she provided that the Agency was not making a case that I had engaged in misconduct by sending

109

personal emails. They were alleging that I had engaged in misconduct because I did not include a disclaimer that I was speaking on behalf of myself as opposed to the government. That aside, she argued that the recipients understood that I was not acting in my official capacity given the context of my emails. In short, she proffered that recipients understood that I was not misusing my position in any way hence the disclaimer was implied.

Ms. McDonough further provided that, "although Lack of Candor does not require intent, it necessarily involves an element of deception." Fargnoli v. Dep't of Commerce, 123 MSPR 330 (May 6, 2016) (citing Ludlum v. Dep't . of Justice, 278 F.3d 1280, 1284–85 (Fed. Cir. 2002) (internal citation omitted)). With that in mind, she argued that the Agency failed to present preponderant evidence of deception because the Agency's only evidence of such was a single comment from May 5, 2019 where they inferred that I told my supervisor that investigators came out to my house in Maryland to interview me in connection with another case where I was a witness to wrongdoing. What I said was something along the lines of, "the investigators came all the way out to me from DC." On that note, Ms. McDonough provided that the Agency's evidence in that regard was insufficient and that it was equipoise. A review of federal case law stipulates that the party with the burden of persuasion has failed to meet its evidentiary burden where the evidence is "equipoise." See e.g., Cook v. Dep't of the Army, 105 MSPR 178 (2007) ("[E]ven if the agency's evidence were equally worthy of belief as that of the appellant, the appellant would be entitled *to prevail."); Knudsen v. Dep't of Health & Human Servs., 35 F.3d 543, 550 (Fed. Cir. 1994).*

Ms. McDonough further provided that the Agency had approved me to work from home at all relevant times as a reasonable accommodation. She explicitly highlighted the following points from my reasonable accommodations order.

> Your physician and therapist both opined that the social stressors of the commute to work exacerbate your conditions; and your symptoms are mitigated when you avoid your known triggers. Therefore, your medical team recommends for you to telework as much as possible in support of your recovery. During the interactive process, you reported that working from home offers you less stimuli and feeling of a safe work environment to avoid your known triggers. You also reported that you mange these symptoms by relaxing (e.g., lying down, taking a nap, etc.). You reported that occasionally you may need to take extended breaks to manage your symptoms should an anxiety attack occur.

> ## Decision

> The medical information establishes the connection between your disability limitations and need for workplace flexibilities. Therefore, based on my review of the information cited above, I approve your request for full-time telework.

With that in mind, she argued that there was no
specific mention of geographic location nor proximity
to the office within the approved order. Ms.
McDonough went on to provide that I worked from
home pursuant to the Agency's reasonable
accommodation order at all relevant times. She also
argued that I could not be held to the standards stated
within the Agency's full-time telework policy because I
had never signed a contract nor order appointing me as
anything beyond a routine teleworker. As such the
Agency's argument that I violated the provisions of the
full-time telework policy were erroneous hence she said
that the charge had to be vacated.

Ms. McDonough also argued that my
termination did not promote the efficiency of the
federal service. Her exact statement was, "to establish
this nexus, an agency must show by a preponderance of
the evidence that the employee's misconduct is likely to
have an adverse effect on the agency's functioning."
Mings v. Dep't of Justice, 813 F.2d 384 (Fed. Cir. 1987).
Furthermore, she provided, "when the MSPB analyzes
whether an agency has shown a nexus between an
employee's misconduct and his/her duties, the board
will consider whether the employee's removal will
protect the integrity of the service as well as whether
she is able to perform the duties of her position."
Doerr v. Office of Personnel Mgmt., 104 MSPR 196 (2006).
On that note, she provided that I had always
performed above the minimally successful level
throughout my career to include periods of extreme
personal stress. Ms. McDonough pulled specific notes

of praise from my performance review to highlight that edict to include:

1. Mr. Moone's performance has exceeded expectations for this performance period. He did an excellent job writing an Executive Business Case for program support. He eagerly took on this assignment, demonstrating an understanding of programmatic objectives, and which resulted in securing funding necessary to achieve organizational goals. His work products are provided in a timely manner and require little revision. He consistently demonstrates his understanding of procurement rules and law."

2. Mr. Moone's performance has exceeded expectations for this performance period. He is proactive in managing activities, providing updates, responding to requests and is able to manage multiple assignments well."

3. Mr. Moone exceeded expectations for this rating period. He worked with various stakeholders across the Agency to develop the acquisition package for Agile Program Services and completed it in a timely manner. He has also been very proactive with managing contracts. He has demonstrated on a consistent basis his understanding of procurement rules and laws.

With all of that in mind, Ms. McDonough said that terminating my employment was counterproductive to the efficiency of the federal service because the Agency had removed a tenured employee with a strong ethic and invaluable enterprise knowledge. She also argued that my termination was unreasonable with respect to the Douglas Factors. The Douglas Factors are a set of 12 standards that must be considered in decisions to discipline federal employees. Those very standards are set by the MSPB. They are as follows:

1. The nature and seriousness of the offense, and its relation to the employee's duties, position, and responsibilities, including whether the offense was intentional or technical or inadvertent, or was committed maliciously or for gain, or was frequently repeated.

2. The employee's job level and type of employment, including supervisory or fiduciary role, contacts with the public, and prominence of the position.

3. The employee's past disciplinary record.

4. The employee's past work record, including length of service, performance on the job, ability to get along with fellow workers, and dependability.

5. The effect of the offense upon the employee's ability to perform at a satisfactory level and its effect upon supervisors' confidence in the employee's work ability to perform assigned duties.

6. Consistency of the penalty with those imposed upon other employees for the same or similar offenses.

7. Consistency of the penalty with any applicable agency table of penalties.

8. The notoriety of the offense or its impact upon the reputation of the agency.

9. The clarity with which the employee was on notice of any rules that were violated in committing the offense or had been warned about the conduct in question.

10. The potential for the employee's rehabilitation.

11. Mitigating circumstances surrounding the offense such as unusual job tensions, personality problems, mental impairment, harassment, or bad faith, malice or provocation on the part of others involved in the matter.

12. The adequacy and effectiveness of alternative sanctions to deter such conduct in the future by the employee or others.

The Wall of Jericho Falls

Ms. McDonough offered counterarguments to everything that Ms. Rain provided with respect to the factors. I will not bother going through all of them however because many of them have already been stated throughout the context of this writing. I will only highlight the most important ones which are factors 1, 2, 5, and 6.

Ms. McDonough provided that the alleged misconduct was not related to the core duties of my position. She also reminded Judge Zamora that the MSPB had long held that Agency's must always consider whether an offense was intentional, technical, or inadvertent. She argued that my mistakes were technical in nature, yet Ms. Rain and Ms. Zenith failed to consider that. They simply decided that my actions were malicious, and they did so without affording me any sort of due process. As such she proffered that it was a mitigating factor. A mitigating factor is, "any fact or circumstance that lessens the severity or culpability of a criminal act." (*Mitigating Factor*).

She also mentioned that while my position was high ranking, it was not one of prominence. As such I had no contact with the public nor true influence. With that in mind she stated that I did not bring any notoriety upon the Agency in effecting their reputation through my actions. The Agency confirmed that that was the case in Discovery. As such this was another mitigating factor.

Ms. McDonough also mentioned that a review of federal cases involving misuse of government equipment showed that personnel typically received multiple warnings and progressive disciplinary action with an exception for extreme cases. An extreme case would be watching or storing porn on a government computer. That was important to note because I did not receive a single warning regarding my email usage.

What's more if you will recall the issue was not that I had misused my equipment, it was simply that I failed to include a disclaimer that I was not speaking on behalf of the government. She also proffered that I used my work email so that I could request read receipts for important and sensitive communication relating to Haelee's life, health, and safety. That was important to note because my personal email account did not possess such functionality. What's more, she also stated that I was preoccupied with concern for my daughter, that circumstances exacerbated my condition thereby affecting my ability to concentrate and impulse control. She argued that I was simply so overwhelmed that I forgot to include the disclaimer under the circumstances. That aside, I took full responsibility for the errors in that regard and I gave a written apology in the filing. Ms. McDonough deemed this as a mitigating factor as well.

Moving along, Ms. McDonough also stated that any representation that management had lost confidence in me was a misrepresentation. This was predicated upon the edict that Ms. Rain became aware of my relocation no later than September 2019. That aside, she made no mention of misconduct nor unsatisfactory performance during my performance reviews [in November 2019 nor May 2020]. Despite all of that, Ms. Rain took it upon herself to recommend me for termination on May 8, 2020. The irony was that she never said a word to me about any misgivings prior to that and that she waited until after I notified her that I would be filing a grievance to recommend me for termination. What was even more ironic was that she continued to allow me to perform my normal duties uninhibited all the way up until my initial termination date of June 5, 2020.

Ms. McDonough concluded our brief by reminding Judge Zamora that I had no history of discipline in the entirety of my career. As such a penalty lesser than termination would have been more appropriate given the context. She also mentioned that both Ms. Zenith and Rain failed to consider lesser penalties and offered no explanations as to why they did not. Ms. McDonough argued that their extreme action in that regard lent credence towards retaliation and discrimination. On that note, she asked Judge Zamora to reverse the removal, reinstate me to my position, award lost wages and benefits, award compensatory damages, award reasonable attorney fees and litigation costs, and other fair and just relief as appropriate.

CHAPTER 12: Go for the Gold

My appeal was unsettled at the time of publication; hence I cannot say whether I won or lost my case. What I do know is that Haelee and I won whether I lose the appeal or not. I won because God did a new thing through us both. She is not only the co-author of this memoir, but she is also the author of the Rules of a Big Boss: A book of self-love. Her book is a personal journey of how she overcame depression, anxieties, and betrayal. It is a manual for young and adult women to maximize higher self-esteem. She also developed a complementary clothing and accessory line in accordance with that book under the name of the Rules of a Big Boss LLC. Those products allow men, women, and children to be as boldly confident as she has now become. With features on ABC 11 News, WRAL 5 News, Spectrum 1 News, Fox 34 News, WBOC 16 News, television shows, print magazines, and podcasts, Haelee's message of empowerment spans across the globe and I have been a witness to it all.

I have been blessed to serve as Haelee's Chief Operating Officer (COO), Manager, and Editor. But not only that, I have become a co-host of an international talk show called TalkTruth Series. The show gives authors and entrepreneurs a platform to elevate their brand by sharing their testimonies. TalkTruth Series broadcasts three days per week via Facebook and YouTube. Haelee and my experiences add validity to the scripture that reads, "But those who hope in the Lord will renew their strength. They will soar on wings like eagles; they will run and not grow weary; they will walk and not be faint." (*The Holy Bible*, Isaiah 40:31, NIV).

Moving along, "God did not promise days without pain, laughter without sorrow, nor sun without rain, but he made a promise: strength for the day, comfort for the tears, and light for the day." (*Taylor 3 Things God Didn't Promise*). God did that very thing for Haelee and I throughout our trials and tribulations. It is almost as if she and I were Shadrach, Meshach, and Abednego, in that we withstood the fiery furnace that was intended to kill us. We survived because God led us out of the furnace. He refined us, redefined us, and is now allowing us to live the purpose-filled life that He set for us. He will do the same thing for you because He loves you so please do not allow yourself to become drowned in despair. He will carry you through all things as He did my daughter and me. He will do so in a way that is especially suited for you. Whatever fire(s) you face, enter the furnace trusting God and watch Him bring you out as gold.

A Word of Prayer

Heavenly Father,

I am grateful for your love. I have been through the furnace, but you were with me. I understand that what the devil meant for evil, you meant for my good. So, God, I close this memoir with gratitude that you never left me to the scorching flames of unemployment, anxiety, or depression. You brought me out of the furnace of dishonest men and a system that would have otherwise destroyed me without your love.

I pray that You will give wisdom to those that are reading this memoir. I pray, Lord, that your tender mercies will be their best companion through each trial they face. It was Jesus who cautioned Peter that the devil sought to sift him as wheat, but Jesus prayed for him. I come in agreement with the name of Jesus Christ and the authority given to Him, that those who read this will come out victorious and will turn again to encourage someone else.

I pray that new strength will be given to them now, in the name of Jesus!

I pray that the flames that try to scorch them will inspire them to press on (because it is only for a season).

I pray that their faith does not fail when trials come.

I pray that their faith does not fail if they get laid off or fired from their jobs.

I pray that their faith does not fail when they get tired of not having enough of what they need.

I pray that their faith does not fail in anything.

Amen.

Dear Reader

I may not know you, but I thank God for you. Let the fire(s) that you go through strip you of every doubt, fear, illness, stress, depression, and everything that would make you otherwise feel defeated. Be purified by your fire(s). No one ever asks for rainy days

122

or cloudy skies, but remember, God is with you through it all. Many have braved the path that you are on and survived, so be encouraged, go in God's grace; Go for the Gold and let the fire be your light.

Appendix 1: Leave Restriction

MEMORANDUM FOR: Mr. Dedrick Moone

Date April 28, 2014

Subject: Leave Restriction

Reference: 220-15-55, Chapter 630 and Chapter 752

1. This memorandum concerns a pattern you have demonstrated of taking unscheduled leave. On Thursday April 10, 2014 you called in sick and Wednesday April 23, 2014 you arrived into the office and ask to take sick leave at 9:00am, you contacted me and advised that you would not be reporting to work because you were "sick and not well." Your need for leave is suspect in that you were sick on days that hot deadlines were due or required meetings with your Supervisor were scheduled. This use of unscheduled leave continues a pattern of such requests commencing on accounts previous sick leave of last year and continuing through the present.

2. Based on a review of your attendance, you are hereby subject to the requirements stated below for reporting to duty, requesting leave

and documenting absences.

    a. Your leave must be requested and approved by me at least two whole workdays in advance of your absence. Approval of leave will be contingent upon whether you have any accrued leave and upon mission requirements.

    b. If circumstances beyond your control (such as injury or other emergency) arise preventing you from reporting to work or from reporting to work on time, I expect you to call me, between 0730 and 0830, to explain the situation. When you call, I further expect that you will indicate the anticipated duration of your absence and request and obtain approval of leave. Calls from individuals acting on your behalf will not be accepted. If, for any reason, I am not available to take your call, you should leave a message concerning your absences and a telephone number where you can be reached. Additionally, you must call me each and everyday of your absence within between 0730 and 0830. As soon as you return to work, you must submit a completed leave request for the period of your absence. Such unscheduled absences should be rare. Depending on the reason and justification for your absence, leave might not be approved, resulting in a charge of Absence without Leave (AWOL.)

3. If you are requesting sick leave (or to substitute annual leave or leave without pay in lieu of sick leave,) of any duration, you must follow the requirements in paragraph (2b). In addition, you must provide your doctor's certification of your absence by having him or her complete a signed statement verifying why you were incapacitated from work and/or why you were unable to report to work (i.e., a diagnosis of your medical condition). Such documentation will not be accepted if it only states, "unable to work" and leave will not be approved. Sick leave requests (or requests for leave without pay (LWOP) in lieu of sick leave will neither be forwarded nor approved by any other staff member without my specific authorization. Sick leave for prearranged medical, dental, or optical examination or treatment must be requested at least one whole workday in advance of your absence. Approval will be contingent upon whether you have accrued sick leave and upon mission requirements and must be subsequently substantiated with medical certification from your physician. You may also be required to provide additional medical documentation of any health condition

should your use of leave not improve, including the history of any medical condition, diagnosis, and prognosis.

4. If you are requesting annual leave (or LWOP in lieu of annual leave) that was not approved in advance of your absence, you must also follow the requirements of paragraph (2b). In addition, upon your return to work you must submit acceptable proof with your written leave request to verify that the emergency or other circumstances beyond your control prevented you from reporting to work. This proof could include a bill for vehicle towing and repairs or any document that provides evidence that the absence was the result of a bona fide emergency which an individual could not reasonably be expected to anticipate. A determination concerning whether an emergency exists and whether leave will be granted will not be made until the documentation described above is received and evaluated.

5. If you do not comply with the above requirements, your absences will be charged to AWOL. AWOL is a non-pay status and will be charged in quarter-hour increments. Although AWOL is not a disciplinary action, you may be subject to discipline for being in AWOL status and/or failure to follow leave procedures.

6. The above procedures are intended to improve your attendance. These leave

procedures will remain in effect for until you have demonstrated marked improvement in your attendance. I will notify you in writing when I have lifted these restrictions. Failure to follow these guidelines during this period will result in disciplinary action up to and including your removal from employment. I trust that you will do whatever is necessary to manage your work schedule and meet your commitments to this office and the mission of this Agency. Your ability to perform as a vital member of our work team is recognized, and your attendance at work on a regular basis is a must for this performance.

7. If personal or health-related problems are contributing to your attendance problems, I strongly urge you to seek help through the Employee Assistance Program (EAP). I am available to assist you in arranging a confidential appointment with a counselor from the EAP at your request, or you may contact the EAP at (800) 222-0365. Use of official duty time to visit the counselor must be coordinated through me.

10. Please sign and date the "Receipt Acknowledgement" line below indicating you have read this notification. Your signature does not indicate your agreement or disagreement with this action. Failure to sign will not void the content of this notice.

11. In addition, all telework privileges are suspended and telework agreement will be

revised.

Acting Chief, KIM
Chief Information

Office

Receipt Acknowledgement:

_____   _____

Signature   Date

Appendix 2: Cease and Desist

MEMORANDUM FOR:

████████████████████

Date: 30 May 2014

Subject: Complaint of
Harassment/Reprisal as Amended 1 June
2014

Reference: Notification and Federal
Employee Antidiscrimination and
Retaliation Act of 2002, Subchapter II,
Chapter 12 of 5 U.S.C. §2302, and §7 of the
Inspector General Act of 1978, as
implemented by DoD Directive 5106.01.

1. This memorandum concerns a pattern
of your continued harassment. I have
recently been subjected to a number of
harmful, offensive, and disruptive actions
which I believe constitute as retaliation,
reprisal, and harassment on your part in
violation of my rights under the
Notification and Federal Employee
Antidiscrimination and Retaliation Act
(No FEAR Act) of 2002. The actions that
I am specifically referring to occurred on

6 May 2014 at approximately 0920, 7 May 2014 at approximately 0825, 12 May 2014 at approximately 1124, 14 May at approximately 1010, 1306, and 1326, 16 May 2014 at 1621, and 29 May at approximately 1657.

2. Such acts are intimidating and repugnant and have had an impact on my daily work. I have not asked for nor do I deserve such hostile treatment. I cannot continue to tolerate such unprofessional conduct going forward.

3. Hence please treat this letter as a formal request to cease and desist such activities going forward. Additionally, if such acts continue, please be advised that I will have no choice but to take additional and necessary steps to protect my rights as an employee and human being.

4. Hopefully, such actions will not be necessary, and we can move forward in a positive direction. Thank you for your attention and cooperation in this matter.

Dedrick Moone
Knowledge Management Lead

133

Office of the Chief Information Officer

Receipt Acknowledgement:

_____   _____

Signature   Date

Appendix 3: Letter to the Superintendent

To: County Superintendent,

Ombudsmen, Board of Education, and

County Delegates

From: Dedrick Moone

Subject: Bullying and Harassment

Good afternoon:

I hope that this email finds you well. With that being said, I feel extremely inclined to reach outto you as a concerned parent of a student. My daughter is an Honor Student at ▮▮▮▮▮▮▮. She is also a Brownie Scout. My daughter has unfortunately been subjected to constant bullying during both school and non-school hours. Her perpetrator is another student at the school who also happens to live four houses down from us. This bullying has consisted of inappropriate touch, foul language (directed at my daughter and myself), threats of violence, acts of physical violence upon my daughter and myself, and several false claims on both school and non-school grounds. I took what I believe to be appropriate proactive measures in notifying the School's Principal, Vice Principal, Guidance Counselor, and Alternative Education Specialist of these issues at onset, August 18, 2015 so as my daughter would be protected and feel safe when she enters school for the day.

As of today, the children have been involved in multiple altercations (21 by my math) during both school and non-school hours. The Administrators at

136

███████████████ failed us failed miserably as they never informed me of the proper procedures to document and report bullying within the school nor community. What's more they never informed me of my rights as a parent, nor citizen. They never made mention of Board of Education POLICY 1060. As a matter of fact, I only found out about the policy in recently conducing my own independent research. They failed to implement prevention procedures with reference towards Bullets E and F of said policy. They have further failed to implement intervention procedures with respect toward Bullets B, C, and F. They have also failed in the area of Reporting procedures with direct reference towards Bullets 3, 4, and 5. They also failed in the area of Violations of Policy with particular reference towards Bullet's 2 A, 2 B, 2 C, 3 D, 7, and 8.

I have spoken with the Director of Elementary Education at the Board of Education regarding out of district transfer requests as this has become much more than an incident of bullying. It has now become a public safety issue. Nevertheless, the School Reassignment Office does not appear willing to treat it as such for some reason or the other. Perhaps they do not believe that things are as bad as they seem. Or perhaps they believe that it is acceptable that my Honor Student and Girl Scout is suffering day in and out when she enters school.

I subsequently reached out to the School Safety Specialist with the State Department of Education as my daughter reiterated to me yet again this morning that she does not want to go to school as she feels unsafe. The School Safety Specialist has been so kind as to listen to my complaints and concerns. He has also reached out to his counterparts within the County in an effort to bring about some form of resolution. Should I have had to elevate these issues to the state?

At any rate, my daughter further reiterated that she does not feel comfortable reporting incidentsof bullying and harassment to the adults due to what I call broken trust. With that in mind, my daughter also informed me that each time she reports any incident between her assailant and herself, her bully goes back to the School Counselor and lies on her so as to make it appear that my daughter was the aggressor while she plays the role of the victim. What's more, my daughter has also reported that her bully has continuously and habitually spread rumors about her. The results of all of these acts have seriously disrupted the learning environment not only for my child but several other students at ████████ What's more is that it has had a significant impacton our day-to-day life. At the end of the day, I am just trying to do the best that I can to protect my daughter as a single parent and father in removing her from this tumultuous environment. However unfortunately as it may be, as mentioned previously it appears that the School Reassignment Office would much rather turn a blind eye towards this public safety and bullying issue. This is extremely concerning to me as a parent as I fear that I and other parents could potentially have other Grace McComas incidents on our hands if something is not done and soon.With that being said, I am reaching out to you in hopes that you might be able to bring about some form of resolution regarding the bullying that is and has been occurring at ███████████ and perhaps facilitate the immediate processing of my out of district transfer request. Please help.

V/r

Dedrick L. Moone
A Humble Man and Father

Appendix 4: Honors Assembly

To: County Superintendent, Ombudsmen,

Board of Education, and County

Delegates

From: Dedrick Moone

Subject: Turned Away from Attending

Honors Assembly

Good morning sir,

I spoke briefly with ████████ ,Principal, ██████████████ regarding the ongoing issues. We have a telephone conference scheduled for Monday at 9:30.

On another note, I'm not certain if you are aware or not, but my daughter is an honor student. She has been as such ever since she was in Pre-K. At any rate, ██████████████ was hosting an assembly today to recognize those students. With that in mind, I have always been a very involved parent in her school activities, functions, and everything that you could imagine as I'm all that she has and vice versa. At any rate, ██████████ advised me that I would not be able to participate in the Honors Ceremony as I am only allowed to drop my daughter off and pick her up. I put no argument up in that regard. Nevertheless, my daughter was fully expecting me to be there as I always have been. I didn't even have an opportunity to inform her that I would not be able to attend after all. Can you imagine how she must feel when she looks back and the one person that's always been there for her isn't there?

Can you imagine how I must feel when the schools beg for parent involvement particularly from that of fathers and I'm disallowed from being able to have lunch with my daughter or even participate in her honor ceremonies?

Please do whatever you can to push the matter through so as my daughter and I may have some peace with regards to her education.

V/r

Dedrick Moone
A Humble and Loving Father

Appendix 5: Letter to President Obama

To: President Barack Obama

From: Dedrick Moone

Subject: Rampant Bullying and Harassment and Lack of Institutional Control Within One of the States "Best" School Systems

Good morning sir,

My daughter and I have been through the ringer in dealing with the school system. My daughter is being bullied & tormented by another child who attends her school & lives in our community. This other child has assaulted my daughter on multiple occasions. She has also attempted to sexually violate my daughter on multiple occasions. She has also spread ungodly rumors about my daughter at school & in our community. The bullying is so out of hand that my daughter is afraid to go to school or even outside & play in our community. To make matters worse is that the other child's parents have stalked, harassed, & threatened her with acts of physical violence, murder, & made mockeries of my disability status. I have spoken with the Board of Education regarding an out of district transfer request for my daughter; however, my pleas to the Superintendent, Board of Education Chairman, etc. have remained unfruitful. As a result, I reached out to State Department of Education regarding these matters. They have been compassionate in their effort to bring forth a resolution yet their hands are tied as they lack executive authority.

I have peace orders in place to protect her from this other child & her parents. Nevertheless, I do not believe that the severity & impact of our sufferings are truly being considered by the school system, State Attorney's Office, nor Juvenile Services. The other child's father has engaged in activities that both violate the in-place peace order & also violate the provisions of the Criminal Code 3-802 & 3-803 in threatening my daughter's life.

The mother has followed suit in also violating the conditions of the peace order & the provisions of Criminal Code 3-804. She has also violated Criminal Code 3-805. With everything being said, I have been living in imminent fear & danger of her life for an extended period of time. As such, we have been staying with a friend & living away from home since 12/29/15 & off/on prior.

What's more, I have also made a judgment decision that I will refrain from sending my daughter to school under the juris of public safety as I do not believe that the school has the capacity to protect her from additional abuse & harm. As a result, I have spoken with the school at length regarding either an out of district transfer &/or home schooling. I have advised them that my daughter will remain home with me until said time that one of my requests are approved. This should not be given that we live in the most civilized nation in the world. Please help her/us.

Sincerely,

V/r

Dedrick L. Moone

Appendix 6: Letter from President Obama

The White House, Washington

Thank you for writing. As President and as a parent, I am committed to combating bullying, harassment, and discrimination in our schools and communities.

Bullying is never acceptable and must not be tolerated. Too often, our children are harassed because of their actual or perceived differences, which we should value rather than target. I am shocked and heartbroken by the losses of young people who took their own lives after being bullied.

My Administration has launched a coordinated effort to prevent suicides and to engage communities in protecting our youth, particularly at-risk groups such as gay, lesbian, bisexual, and transgender youth. In August 2010, we held the first-ever National Bullying Summit, which brought together State, local, tribal, civic, and corporate leaders to share perspectives and plan a national strategy to take on bullying. We must ensure young Americans can learn in safe environments and can find and receive help from caring adults. To learn more about my Administration's commitment to addressing bullying and to find resources, please visit www.StopBullying.gov.

We know government alone cannot bring an end to these troubling incidents. Combating bullying and harassment requires us to create a sustained and serious dialogue, and to engage institutions and individuals across our country. Every adult has an obligation to set an example of respect and compassion, and to reject all forms of discrimination.

Thank you again, for writing.

Sincerely,

Barack Obama

Visit WhiteHouse.gov

Appendix 7: Letter from the US Department of Education

January 5, 2016
WH-20160105-06780308

Dear Dedrick Moone

Thank you for your letter to President Barack
Obama regarding your daughter being bullied. The
White House has referred your letter to the U. S.
Department of Education's Office for Civil Rights
(OCR), Customer Service Team for reply, and I am
pleased to respond.

OCR enforces several Federal civil rights laws
that prohibit discrimination in programs or
activities that receives Federal financial assistance
from the Department; in addition to many public
schools, colleges and universities, and some
private and parochial schools also are recipients
of Federal financial assistance from the
Department. These laws are:

- Title VI of the Civil Rights Act of 1964, on
  the bases of race, color, or national origin.
- Title IX of the Education Amendments of
  1972, on the basis of sex.
- Section 504 of the Rehabilitation Act of 1973,
  on the basis of disability.
- and the Age Discrimination Act of 1975, on
  the basis of age.

OCR also enforces Title II of the Americans with
Disabilities Act of 1990, which prohibits discrimination
on the basis of disability by public entities, whether or
not they receive Federalfinancial assistance.

OCR also enforces the Boy/Girl Scouts of America

Equal Access Act, which addresses equalaccess to school facilities for the Boy Scouts and certain other youth groups.

OCR's enforcement offices investigate complaints of alleged discrimination filed with the Department. Please keep in mind, however, that complaints must be filed with OCR within 180 calendar days of the alleged discrimination to be considered filed in a timely manner. Determination of subject matter jurisdiction and determination of whether OCR has jurisdiction over the institution alleged to have committed discrimination are initial steps in complaint investigation.

I am forwarding your discrimination complaint with OCR's Atlanta Enforcement Office (Atlanta Office). The Atlanta Office is responsible for investigations of educational institutions in Georgia and provides technical assistance.

If you wish, you may also contact the Atlanta Office directly at the following address andtelephone numbers:

Office for Civil Rights, Atlanta Office
U.S. Department of Education
61 Forsyth St. S.W., Suite 19T10
Atlanta, GA 30303-8927
Telephone: 404-974-9406
Fax: 404-974-9471

TTY: 800-877-8339
Email: OCR.Atlanta@ed.gov

You may file a complaint with OCR, online, at: http://www.ed.gov/about/offices/list/ocr/docs/ho wto.html.

Also, that web site includes the How to File a Discrimination Complaint with the Office for Civil Rights pamphlet, which explains the kind of information that is needed in filing a complaint and the OCR: Ensuring Equal Access to High-Quality Education pamphlet, at: http://www.ed.gov/about/offices/list/ocr/docs/ens ure03.html.

In addition, on October 26, 2010, the Department issued guidance to support educators in combating bullying in schools by clarifying when student bullying may violate federal educationanti-discrimination laws at: http://www.ed.gov/news/press-releases/guidance-targeting- harassment-outlines-local-and-federal-responsibility .

The civil rights laws represent a national commitment to end discrimination in educational programs. The laws also work toward promoting the Department's mission to promote studentachievement and preparation for global competitiveness by fostering educational excellence and ensuring equal access.

I hope this information provi0ded is of assistance to you.

Sincerely,

Tamara Merges
Customer Service Team
Office for Civil Rights

Appendix 8: Reasonable Accommodations Denied

May 5, 2020

MEMORANDUM FOR   DEDRICK MOONE

Project Specialist

FROM:

SUBJECT: Reasonable Accommodation - FINAL DECISION

In 2015, you were approved a modified work schedule and special work space seating as a reasonable accommodation. In 2016, you reported that your symptoms had worsened and the accommodation was no longer effective. On June 14, 2016, I approved your request for full-time telework.

On September 28, 2017, the Office of Human Resources Management (OHRM) requested medical information for an annual review of your accommodation needs. Because of a supervisory change, on March 17, 2019, Director, Program Management Division, began managing your work and your accommodation.

155

██████████████ left the agency on March 20, 2020. I am now the appropriate deciding official for this matter.

Despite the fact that, in your 2016 accommodation decision, you were given notice of that such annual reviews could occur, you have resisted the agency's efforts to review and manage your reasonable accommodation needs. You contended that the agency's request was over-reaching and in violation of your disability rights. The agency requested the medical review because your medical information was stale. The agency needs updated medical information to confirm your current symptoms and limitations, and how they are affecting your ability to perform your job duties.

Both the Americans with Disabilities Act Amendments Act (ADM) and Reasonable Accommodation Policy, HRM 2300.1, require employees to cooperate with the interactive process, including responding to the agency's request for medical information. According to OHRM, the ADM allows the agency to conduct a medical inquiry that is job-related and consistent with business necessity; and, as necessary, to determine the need for an accommodation, and the most effective accommodations to grant, if any.

OHRM made repeated requests for new medical information and addressed your questions and concerns about the need for new medical information. Despite the agency's efforts, from September 28, 2017 to July 8, 2019, you caused significant delays and continued to resist participating in a necessary element of the reasonable accommodation interactive process.

OHRM informed you that the ADAAA specifically allows the agency to deny accommodations when employees do not produce and/or fail to cooperate with a reasonable medical inquiry.

Order HRM 2300.1 provides, in Section 2, 7c, provides that the requester's failure to provide appropriate documentation or to cooperate in efforts to obtain such documentation may result in a denial of reasonable accommodation.

During this process ███████████ learned, not from you but from other sources that you had relocated to the North Carolina area and were working remotely from there since 2016. You did so without requesting or receiving permission. You were granted full-time telework in June 2016 on the basis that you suffered from a disabling condition that caused severe panic attacks; impaired your ability to cope with the congestion of commuting from Maryland to Washington, DC; and that you were receiving intense psychotherapy twice a week; and that you were visiting your psychiatrist once per month, as needed for medication management. I also approved the flexibility of taking periodic breaks and working an irregular work schedule to allow for your twice a week appointments (that conflicted with business hours) and to help you manage your triggers and symptoms. Granting you those flexibilities caused significant disruption of work demands, meetings with stakeholders, and presentations you were responsible for facilitating. It was therefore critical to re-evaluate your prognosis and need for continued accommodations. Furthermore, after granting you a reasonable accommodation to suit your care and treatment in the Washington, DC area, your lack of transparency around your relocation to North Carolina legitimately raised questions and concerns about your accommodation needs, among other things.

Given the contentious and protracted nature of obtaining medical information from you, on May 30, 2019, OHRM determined it was best to seek review of your condition by an independent medical provider at the Department of Health and Human Services, Federal Occupational Health Division (FOH). After 22 months of the agency's efforts, on July 8, 2019, you consented to the requested FOH review.

After reviewing additional medical records obtained from your providers and consultation with at least two providers, FOH made an initial report on November 18, 2019, and a supplemental report on January 21, 2020. FOH confirmed that you sporadically visit with your therapist for an anxiety disorder that causes difficulty interacting with others, and that your condition appears to be stable with periodic periods of exacerbation and improvement. According to your therapist, she is not aware of any problems of you performing your job duties as long as you work from home. Your therapist, however, noted that your resistance to working in Washington, DC may be due to you being a single parent. FOH learned that your therapist does not coordinate care and does not have contact information for your psychiatrist.

FOH did, however, consult with your psychiatrist who reported that he treated you in the hospital from June 24 to 29, 2019, and did not notice that you had any impairment in driving and performing normal daily life activities. Your psychiatrist specifically stated, "I do not believe [he) has any limitations in his ability to interact with others. I did not see [that] he has any health conditions to prevent him from traveling to Washington, DC." Your psychiatrist also had no knowledge of the reasons why you live in North Carolina when your job is located in Washington, DC.

FOH noted that your medical information was vague about the reasons you need to telework full-time because of social anxiety but you are able to otherwise perform your Project Manager job duties. Given the limited medical information and encounters with your providers, FOH stated, "It appears that there may be important non-medical reasons for Mr. Moone to try to work from..." Finally, FOH found that your providers did not present any medical information to support that you suffer from a disabling medical condition that requires an accommodation.

It is also important to note that, from the start of OHRM's September 28, 2017 request for new medical information, you reported that your provider was unwilling to address the medical inquiry because she believed it was an overreach, was a violation of HIPPA, would be detrimental to her continued career status, and because your conditions had not materially changed since 2016. In fact, on February 28, 2018, you reported to OHRM that your provider terminated you from her practice for these reasons. The agency has come to learn, however, that you terminated your treatment with this Maryland-based provider when you elected to relocate to North Carolina in 2016.

You reported to OHRM that your provider (whom you said had terminated you from her practice) referred you to another doctor. You stated that your new provider needed time to assess your condition and needs. At the time OHRM was unaware of your relocation and granted you further extensions to allow time for your new doctor to assess you.

Thereafter, on each occasion when OHRM followed up, you gave reasons for further delay and resisted cooperation. Finally, the records show that, when you relocated to North Carolina in 2016, you apparently abandoned the intense twice-a-week psychotherapy visits and the monthly visits with your psychiatrist established for you in 2016, Not once during this process, however, did you comply with the repeated requests for a re-evaluation of your medical needs and accommodation needs. Neither did you offer any medical reasons for relocating to North Carolina in 2016.

Interim Accommodations .
Since September 28, 2017, OHRM engaged in efforts to re-evaluate your current medical limitations and need

160

for accommodation. Despite the significant delays you caused and your continued resistance to the process, your supervisor continued to allow for you to telework full-time, without disruption.

Decision

While the medical information confirmed your medical condition, it did not sufficiently establish that you suffer from limitations that required a need to relocate to North Carolina for medical care and treatment, and thus, full-time remote work is required to accommodate your symptoms by enabling you to perform the essential functions of your job. In fact, FOH discovered in its review that there were no medical limitations to you traveling and working in Washington, DC. When, on June 14, 2016, I approved your telework accommodation, I provided notice that your accommodation would be subject to annual reviews. Specifically, I stated: "Your reasonable accommodation may be re-evaluated with a request for medical information after March 31, 2017, to confirm the state of your current limitations, to include, if the essential functions of your job change, and/or if your medical conditions change. Please be advised that you are obligated to keep me apprised of any changes in your medical condition that may warrant a change in your accommodation needs."

For 22 months you failed to cooperate with an essential element of the reasonable accommodation process despite the many efforts to engage you and to re-evaluate your current medical limitations and need for accommodation. Finally, after a complete medical review, FOH found that there are likely personal, and not medical, reasons for you living in North Carolina and declining to work in Washington, DC, where your assigned duty station is located.

FOH also found that your providers did not present any medical information demonstrating that you suffer from a disabling medical condition that requires an accommodation. For these reasons, I terminate your full-time telework accommodation.

Under the circumstances, you may be eligible for up to 12 weeks or 480 hours intermittent or consecutive of unpaid leave during any 12-month calendar period under the Family and Medical Leave Act (FMLA). You may elect to substitute annual leave and/or sick leave for any unpaid leave under the FMLA. See link below

https://www.opm.gov/policy-data-oversight/pay-leave/leave-administration/fact-sheets/family-and-medical-leave/

You will need your doctor to complete the attached medical certificate and return it to me. Once approved, your leave will be recorded as FMLA annual, sick or LWOP.

Around March 16, 2020, the Administrator mandated telework for staff in support of the state and local government's Public Health Emergency Stay-At-Home Orders. In accordance with the agency's telework mandate you may telework from Washington, DC. Please understand that once the agency's COVID-19

162

Policy is lifted you will be expected to return to a regularly assigned work schedule at ███████████████ Washington, DC 20405, that includes two (2) telework days per week. Please feel free to contact me at the earliest to establish your newly assigned tour of duty which will need to be changed in HR Links.

If you are dissatisfied with this decision, you may request reconsideration of this decision within seven (7) business days from receipt of this decision to ███████████ Assistant Commissioner, ████████████████████████████

INSTRUCTION FOR RECONSIDERATION OF DECISION

If an individual wishes to request reconsideration of this decision, take the following steps:

Ask the decisionmaker to reconsider denial. Additional information may be presented to support this request.

If the decisionmaker was the individual's supervisor, the individual can ask a higher level manager in the chain of command to review the decision.

If the decision is not overturned, the individual may file an Equal Employment Opportunity (EEO) complaint, or pursue Merit System Protection Board (MSPB) or union grievance (collective bargaining claim) procedures. To do this, take the following steps:

For an EEO complaint pursuant to 29 CFR Part 1614, contact the EEO officer in your appropriate area within 45 calendar days from the date of the decision.

For a collective bargaining claim, file a written grievance according to the provisions of the Collective Bargaining Agreement.

For a MSPB appeal submit the request within 30 days of an appealable adverse action as defined in 5 CFR Part 1201.3.

Appendix 9: Appeal Follow-up

From: Dedrick Moone

To: ███████████

Bcc: ████████████████

Date: Friday, May 8, 2020 at 10:44 AM

Hi ██████████

I understand that you are extremely busy. With that being said, I wanted to take an opportunity to thank you for taking the time out of your schedule to speak with me not only once but twice.

Moving along I am not certain that I was clear in my request. As such, I thought it worthwhile to follow-up so to speak. As stated, I am not exactly asking that a decision in allowing me to work remotely be overturned. I am actually asking for a little more than that. I would like to be allowed to do my job remotely while no longer reporting to ████████████. The reason being is mistrust which will be outlined in the text to follow. ██████████ made a reference towards unsatisfactory performance in reaching her decision to deny my reasonable accommodations. She specifically stated, "Granting you those flexibilities caused significant disruption of work demands, meetings with stakeholders, and presentations you were responsible for facilitating. It was therefore critical to re-evaluate your prognosis and need for continued accommodations" in her decision letter dated May 5, 2020. That in itself is extremely concerning to me as decision letter was the first time that I have heard of such performance problem one of these items were or have been noted in any of my performance evaluations.

166

Moving along, another item of note has been ███████ ██████ continued insistence of wholly invasive information with respect to my health file. That in and of itself stretches back to February 2016. Please see the document entitled Moone, Dedrick RMI as a point of reference. My former therapist advised me that the information request was over the top in that ███████ ██ need only know my diagnosis, stressors, and prognosis to make a determination regarding accommodations under the provisions of the ADA Amendments Act of 2008 particularly where I had not signed a HIPPA Medical Release Request at that time. Notwithstanding ████████ complied with the request in answering the questions at a very high level not once but twice. ███ ██████ had to do it twice because ██████████ stated that her initial letter did not address all of her concerns. A copy of both letters is attached. The first one is entitled DMoone Reasonable Accommodations Letter 02252016, while the second one is entitled DMoone Reasonable Accommodations Letter 03012016. ███ ██████ advised me that it was not in my best interest to sign a HIPPA Medical Release because it contained information related to not only myself but my underage daughter and her mother. She advised that she couldn't pick and choose what she sent over in the event of my signing off on the HIPPA Medical Release Request. To that end, she would have to send over everything. persistent invasiveness led towards ██████████ eventually dropping me as a patient. My daughter and I had a long term relationship with her hence you can imagine that that was damaging to my mental health. I did however eventually sign a HIPPA Medical Release on November 20, 2019 under guise and coercion. Another important item of note was that I was completely unaware of a stipulation that required me to reside in the Washington, DC Metro Area. The reason being is that it was never stated to me verbally or in any type of Agency Designated Literature. This can be affirmed by taking a look at the document entitled RA Decision - DM 6 - 14 - 16 (2). What's more I do not and never had an official position description of my actual position of record as a Contracts Manager. All that I ever had was an unofficial position description.

As stated previously, there were extenuating circumstances that precipitated my decision to relocate. Those extenuating circumstances were the mental and physical health/safety of not only my child and I. I am not certain if all of this presents a problem with respect to regional pay or not but I am willing to make restitution as/if necessary.

I love working at ████. As such I would love to continue and finish out my career with the Agency. I simply want to be able to do my job virtually without fear of retribution/reprisal, interference, and repeated invasive requests for my medical information particularly where OHRM instruction previously provided that "Your reasonable accommodation may be re-evaluated with a request for medical information after March 31, 2017, to confirm the state of your current limitations, to include, if the essential functions

Moone/The Unexpected Journey

of your job change, and/or if your medical conditions change."

Thank you again for the opportunity to not only chat but appeal. All of the best.

V/r

--

4 attachments

RA Decision - DM 6-14-16 (2).pdf

174K

DMoone Reasonable Accommodation Letter 030116.PDF

131K

Moone/The Unexpected Journey

Moone_Dedrick_RMI II_2016-02-16 (1).pdf

227K

DMoone Reasonable Accommodation Letter
022616.PDF

102K

Appendix 10: Victim Impact Statement

Bottom Line Upfront

Working with ███████████ can be difficult because she presents one course and performs the complete opposite. For example, on May 5, 2020 she reported that she wanted to revoke my accommodations with my working in the office three days per week. That is/was most concerning to me because it has long been documented that the commute to and from Washington, DC is one of my triggers. That trigger in itself is further compounded in the midst of a global pandemic (COVID-19). I submitted the complaint that we are discussing [at present] on May 6, 2020 as a result of everything. ███████████ illegally retaliated by recommending me for termination on May 11, 2020. It is unreasonable and unethical to request someone to return to the office, but just a week later recommend them for termination. Moreover, ███████████ continued to assign work projects to me for completion even after she reported that she was unable to trust me.

I have been suffering from insomnia as a result of ███████████ and ███████████ callous, discriminatory, and retaliatory actions. I have only been getting three to four hours of sleep per night since ███████████ submitted her resignation on March 20, 2020. That led to ███████████ becoming my first line supervisor again. I have been experiencing loss of appetite to the point that I am only eating once per day if at all. What's more I been suffering from increased irritability and lack of patience. This has led to increased social isolation. This has negatively affected my ability to parent my daughter. That has caused her to grow up sooner than she otherwise should in that she has been forced to become more independent in not only caring for herself, but me as well. I am also suffering from increased feelings of hopelessness and decreased sexual desire. This has also led to my beginning to drink alcoholic beverages. This is of utmost importance because I did not drink prior to this. I have begun to do so however to help me cope with matters as a result of everything that ████████ ██████ and ██████████████████████ have done to me over the past few months and several years.

Everything leads me to wonder what my healthy path is going forward with respect to what ████████████ ████████████████████████ have done and have allowed to happen to me.

Background

My name is Dedrick Moone and I suffer from anxiety, agoraphobia, panic, and depression.

While I do not remember the exact date of occurrence or diagnosis, these conditions appeared sometime in 2014. These conditions were brought upon by working in a hostile work at ████████████████████ ████████████

173

██████████. I sought treatment at ████████
Hospital to treat those conditions.

I began working at ████ as a Project Manager on July
27, 2014. It was a scary proposition for me because I
never worked in a city as big as Washington, DC.
Notwithstanding I believed that I could handle working
in the city because I needed to. I saw ████ as an escape
of sorts.

I began to experience complications with the
conditions in January 2015. The complications were
predicated upon the daily commute to work and the
open office concept nature of ████ Those
complications led to my having a panic attack at ██████
Headquarters in July 2015. I believed that I was going
to die because I experienced shortness of breath,
tightness in my chest, and lightheadedness among other
things. My then supervisor, ██████████, Director
Governance sent me to the Infirmary to help me
recover. I felt embarrassed, defeated, ashamed, and
afraid in large because this occurred at work. I
resultantly wondered who witnessed what had
happened after my then colleagues saw me in a prone
position. I also wondered how things would look if it
happened again in either the near or distant future.
Better yet, I wondered what ██████████ would think
of me going forward and the impact that it would have
on my continued career.

I began intensive therapeutic intervention with ██████
██████████ immediately thereafter. She and my

PCP suggested that I make a request for Reasonable Accommodation for fulltime telework in light of my worsening condition(s) and environmental triggers. I followed up in making that specific request in January 2016. ███████████ advised that my position required that I be onsite hence she could not accommodate me. She said what she could do instead was work to find a position that would. ███████████ found a position for me as a Contracts Manager under ███████████, Director PMO. She stated that the position could accommodate me in that it did not require me to work onsite. Notwithstanding she stated that I would still have to fill out the official paperwork to request Reasonable Accommodations. I did so in making that specific request on February 4, 2016 to ███████ ███████ She in turn sent the information to ███████ ███████████, Reasonable Accommodations Coordinator. transmitted a Request for Medical Information (RMI) on February 16, 2016 ███████ ███████████ was extremely concerned about the information being requested as she stated that it was overreach. My provider specifically stated then that the information being requested could be used against me in an attempt to destroy my career particularly where ███████████ and ███████████ were inquiring about my functional limitations, affected life activities, and prescribed medications to include their side effects. ███████████ specifically stated that she could not provide that depth of information without my signing a medical release document. What's more, she advised me to refrain from signing a medical release and that she would answer the questions at a very high level. Answering the questions at a high level protected my personal medical background but skirted the lines of what was medically ethical. ██████████████████████ transmitted her response on February 25, 2016. ████████████████ and ███████████████████████, stated that the letter was insufficient, so they requested additional information. That of course raised my anxiety as I believed then that they were going to attempt to say that I was incapable of doing the job. Notwithstanding I took the request for additional information back to my provider. My provider reluctantly complied with the request to provide additional data on March 1, 2016. ██████████████████████ again stated that complying with ███████████████ and ████████████████ ██████████ requests could potentially endanger their licensure. Given that premise she informed me that she would not comply with any additional RMI's unless I was willing to take a chance on signing a medical release form. She also advised that I should consider hiring an attorney. I declined to do so because I wanted to trust that ████████████ and █████████████-██████████ were operating in good faith. I unfortunately found out time and again that they were not. ███████████████, █████████████████████████, and I had several meetings after I submitted that second letter. ████████████ and ████████████████ ██████████ continued to overreach in continuing to request the information that my provider could not legally provide without my signing off on a medical release. Those meetings had to be cut short because I became panicked and had anxiety attacks each time. I began to mistrust ███████████ and ████████ ████████████████ immediately thereafter with respect to my mental health because they put me in those positions unnecessarily with no apologies. ████████ █████████ in particular displayed a complete lack of empathy in seeing me in such a prone condition. Notwithstanding they subsequently decided to afford the accommodation of fulltime telework on June 14, 2016. The written agreement stipulated that I would not have to go through the process again unless either my job changed, or my health condition improved. ████████████████████████████ on the other hand verbally informed me that the information that I provided would be placed within my HR File such that I would not have to go through the process again given my longstanding history of disability and the fact that doing so puts me in a compromising position. ██████████ ███████████ was promoted to the position of Deputy Assistant Commissioner on or around August 2017. ████████████████ was subsequently promoted to ██████████████ former position. █████████████████ stated that she advised ██████████████ that I had Reasonable Accommodations and that I would need to work with both her and ████████████████████ to get them recertified. ████████████████████ sent me a letter on September 28, 2017 wherein she essentially requested the same information that she and ████████████ had requested previously. That of course increased my degree of mistrust. ██████ ████████████████ refused to comply ████████ ██████ and █████████████████████ abated their request once I conveyed that information to them. That aside, my mental health was now in jeopardy as I then had to find and build a relationship with a new medical provider. I felt completely violated in large because I had to suffer from increased irritability, insomnia, social detachment, depression, etc. on my own without the assistance of a treating provider.

I found a new provider in late 2017. I gave her a copy of the RMI dated September 28, 2017. She concurred with ██████████████████████ that the information being requested was overreaching. What's more she advised that they too would not have complied nor would they comply without my signing a medical release. ██████████████ further affirmed that releasing too much information related to my condition and treatment could be damaging to my career. That all increased my anxiety yet again as I feared that my upstanding and dedicated career might be in jeopardy. Notwithstanding I took some solace in knowing that would help me manage my conditions.

Moving along, ███████████████████████ began to request that same information and data yet again in or around June 2019. I inquired would it be possible for ████████████ to provide a limited release of data wherein she could simply state that there had been no change to my medical condition and that I still required accommodations. ██████████████████ stated that that was not permissible, and that ████████████ would have to provide all of the information requested. I reminded █████████████████████ that I lost my previous provider due to their overreach and that I was not going to allow it to happen again with everything being considered. I then offered to allow myself to be subjected to an independent neurological assessment with a provider of her choosing as a concession. What that meant is that I was willing to go to a provider of ████████████████ and ████████████ choosing and let them perform a diagnosis. ████████ ██████████████████ was accepting of that offer. She stated that I would have to sign off on a medical release so as the independent physician could compare notes with my current and former providers. I signed off on that medical release on July 8, 2019, November 19, 2019, and again on November 20, 2019 with the understanding that ██████████████████████ would be setting up an appointment for an independent assessment. Nothing else was said to me about my Reasonable Accommodations or RMI until May 5, 2020 when ██████████████ made the decision to revoke my Reasonable Accommodations. I appealed the decision to ████████████ on May 6, 2020. I spoke with ██████████████ in detail on both May 7 and May 8, 2020 regarding matters. ██████████████ transmitted a letter on May 22, 2020 wherein she upheld ██████████ egregious and callous decisions. ████████████ would have been the deciding official with regards to my Reasonable Accommodations; however, she submitted her resignation effective March 20, 2020 █████████ made the decision that she would serve as both the Deputy Assistant Commissioner and Director PMO as opposed to temporarily promoting someone. I have suffered from increased anxiety and depression since said time. The reason being is that ████████████ creates a toxic work environment. That results and resulted in an abundance of undo stress and anxiety. I subsequently started looking for other opportunities within the Agency. I did so not only because of the undo anxiety but because of mistrust in ████████ ████████ given the previous experiences in her attempting to gather potentially damaging medical data on myself and [possibly] my family.

Appendix 11: Recission of Decision to Remove

Via Electronic Mail Transmission

July 9, 2020

Dedrick Moone

Re: Rescission of Decision to Remove

Dear Mr. Moone:

The purpose of this letter is to inform you that the decision to remove letter dated June 5, 2020, is hereby rescinded. A revised proposal letter, Douglas Factor analysis, and evidence file will be reissued to you. The revised proposal letter will include a new notice period and another opportunity for you to reply.

Your employment with ■■■ will be reinstated during this period effective June 8, 2020, and you will receive appropriate back-pay, benefits, and other emoluments.

Sincerely,

Works Cited

"14 CFR § 302.22 - Prehearing Conference." *Legal Information Institute*, Legal Information Institute, https://www.law.cornell.edu/cfr/text/14/302.22 .

"Anxiety Disorders." *National Institute of Mental Health*, U.S. Department of Health and Human Services, www.nimh.nih.gov/health/topics/anxiety-disorders/index.shtml.

"AWOL." *Merriam-Webster.com Dictionary*, Merriam-Webster, https://www.merriam-webster.com/dictionary/AWOL. Accessed 28 Dec. 2020.

Daniel K. Hall-Flavin, M.D. "Nervous Breakdown: What Does It Mean?" *Mayo Clinic*, Mayo Foundation for Medical Education and Research, 26 Oct. 2016, http://www.mayoclinic.org/diseases-conditions/depression/expert-answers/nervous-breakdown/faq-20057830.

Federal Sector Alternative Dispute Resolution Fact Sheet. (n.d.). Retrieved from https://www.eeoc.gov/federal-sector/federal-sector-alternative-dispute-resolution-fact-sheet

Hill, Gerald N., and Kathleen Hill. *The People's Law Dictionary: Taking the Mystery out of Legal Language.* MJF Books, 2002.

"HIPAA Release Form." *HIPAA Journal*, 16 July 2020, www.hipaajournal.com/hipaa-release-form/.

The Holy Bible. NIV ed., Biblica, 2011.

How Much Does an Employment Discrimination Lawsuit Cost? (n.d.). Retrieved from https://personalfinance.costhelper.com/employ ment-discrimination-lawsuit.html

Ivancie, Mike. "The Douglas Factors Explained, the Keys to a Discipline Case." *Ivancie Law*, 28 Oct. 2017, www.ivancielaw.com/federal-employment-law/what-are-the-douglas-factors/.

"Lazy Eye (Amblyopia)." *Mayo Clinic*, Mayo Foundation for Medical Education and Research, 7 Aug. 2019, www.mayoclinic.org/diseases-conditions/lazy-eye/symptoms-causes/syc-20352391.

McNicholas, C., Poydock, M., & Rhinehart, L. (2019). *The Trump NLRB's attack on workers' rights* (Rep.). Washington, District of Columbia: Economic Policy Institute. Retrieved December 19, 2020, from https://www.epi.org/publication/unprecedented -the-trump-nlrbs-attack-on-workers-rights/.

"Mitigating Factor." *Legal Information Institute*, Legal Information Institute, http://www.law.cornell.edu/wex/mitigating_fact or.

Ogrysko, N. (2019, May 14). Despite court decision, unions still feel impacts of Trump's workforce executive orders. Retrieved from https://federalnewsnetwork.com/unions/2019/05/despite-court-decision-unions-still-feel-impacts-of-trumps-workforce-executive-orders/

Ogrysko, N. (2019, October 04). With injunction lifted, OPM tells agencies to implement Trump's workforce executive orders. Retrieved December 19, 2020, from https://federalnewsnetwork.com/workforce/2019/10/with-injunction-lifted-opm-tells-agencies-to-implement-trumps-workforce-executive-orders/

"Questions and Answers: No FEAR Act." *U.S. Equal Employment Opportunity Commission,* https://www.eeoc.gov/no-fear/questions-and-answers-no-fear-act.

Sara McDonough. (2020, May 07). Retrieved December 26, 2020, from https://www.dcemploymentattorney.com/about-us/our-team/sara-mcdonough/

Tamara L. Slater. (2019, August 19). Retrieved December 26, 2020, from https://www.dcemploymentattorney.com/about-us/our-team/tamara-slater/

Taylor, LeeAnn G. "3 Things God Didn't Promise." *LeeAnn G Taylor - Embracing the Mosaic Life,* 24 Feb. 2014, leeanngtaylor.com/3-things-god-didnt-promise/.

185

Team, B. (2017, April 06). Legal Brief - Definition, Examples, Cases, Processes. Retrieved December 26, 2020, from https://legaldictionary.net/legal-brief/

Top Rated Washington, DC Employment Litigation Attorney: Sara McDonough. (2018, January 9). Retrieved December 26, 2020, from https://profiles.superlawyers.com/washington-dc/washington/lawyer/sara-n-mcdonough/6ce415fe-1f05-42f7-8426-f27bc6654de7.html

U.S. Merit Systems Protection Board - About. (n.d.). Retrieved from https://www.mspb.gov/About/about.htm

U.S. Merit Systems Protection Board - Prohibited Personnel Practices. (n.d.). Retrieved from https://www.mspb.gov/ppp/9ppp.htm

UNITED STATES OF AMERICA MERIT SYSTEMS PROTECTION BOARD Washington Regional Office. *Dedrick Moone Vs Agency.* 15 Jan. 2021.

UNITED STATES OF AMERICA MERIT SYSTEMS PROTECTION BOARD Washington Regional Office. *Dedrick Moone Vs Agency.* 10 Dec. 2020.

What Is a Motion to Compel? - Discovery Law Explained. 28 Jan. 2020, valientemott.com/blog/motion-to-compel/.

Wheeler, T. (2020, March 15). Trigger Point Injection (TPI) for Muscle Pain Relief. Retrieved from https://www.webmd.com/pain-management/guide/trigger-point-injection

Acknowledgements

I would like to thank God first and foremost. He has kept me through all seasons through His sufficiency's, grace, and mercy.

I would like to recognize my daughter, Haelee P. Moone for helping me write this memoir. I would also like to acknowledge her for giving me the strength to reveal myself and share my story.

I would like to acknowledge and recognize my granny, Beulah M. Moone. You are my forever best friend and spiritual advisor. You prayed for me [daily] when I was not strong nor wise enough to do so for myself. It took me several years to understand the impetus behind your famous words of, "baby be strong." I now understand that you were imploring me to press toward the goal to win the prize. I carry that message with me daily and I specifically carried it with me as I retold my story through this writing. May you continue to Rest in Heavenly Peace.

I would like to honor my mom, Wanda R. Moone. You have always been there whenever I was at my lowest. That has afforded me the luxury of a place to call home in all circumstances.

I would like to honor Terence G. Westry for simply being an inspiration and a father.

I would like to recognize and thank Dr. Vanessa J. Raynor for being my most loving and dedicated friend. You have picked me up when I was down, encouraged me to fight forward, never give up, and ensured that I always had a word on my heart. Not only that but you also served as a sounding board for my diatribes when no one else cared to hear them.

I would like to thank SherriAnita A. Pitts, Andrea N. Spence, and DeOnna S. Pierce for being my closest friends, sounding boards, adopted sisters, and keeping me laughing and encouraged throughout the years.

I would like to acknowledge Karen B. Tyson, Genesis, A. Kemp, Shanique MJ Davis, and Kiescha Cherry for serving as my accountability partners, sounding boards, friends, and brand ambassadors.

I would like to acknowledge and honor Sterling M. Harrell for his graphic designs.

I would also like to acknowledge and honor my Moonebeams family as well. Your efforts did not go unnoticed by any means as many of them contributed towards the development of this memoir.

I would like to honor Pastor Rodgers for allowing me to be a frequent visitor at Cedar Point Disciples of Christ Church.

I unfortunately do not have enough space to acknowledge everyone. But do know that you are appreciated and loved.

Contact Us

You can connect or contact us via either social media or the web. Details are provided below. We hope to hear from you.

	https://www.thebookofselflove.com
	@thebookofselflove2020
	@thebookofselflove2020
	@The Rules of a Big Boss

www.ingramcontent.com/pod-product-compliance
Lightning Source LLC
Chambersburg PA
CBHW070639150426
42811CB00050B/385